Lyric of Silence

Lyric of Silence

Jaiya John

Soul Water Rising

Camarillo, California

Lyric of Silence: A Poetic Telling of the Human Soul Journey

Copyright © 2010 by Jaiya John

All rights reserved under International and Pan-American Copyright Conventions.

No part of this book may be reproduced or transmitted in any form or by any means electronic or mechanical including photocopying, recording, or by any information storage and retrieval system, without permission in writing from the publisher, except by a reviewer, who may quote brief passages in a review. Address inquiries to books@soulwater.org.

Printed in the United States of America

Soul Water Rising
Camarillo, California
http://www.soulwater.org

Library of Congress Control Number: 2010914933
ISBN 978-0-9916401-6-4

First Soul Water Rising Softcover Edition: 2016

Poetry | Spirituality | Philosophy

Editors:
Jacqueline V. Richmond
Kent W. Mortensen

Cover design & photo: Jaiya John
Interior design & artwork: Jaiya John

Silence is a source of great strength.
—Lao Tzu

We need silence to be able to touch souls.
—Mother Teresa

A day of Silence can be a pilgrimage in itself.
—Hafiz

Much silence makes a powerful noise.
—African proverb

INTRODUCTION

Welcome, Soul. The words that follow are not poems. Not in the sense of independent bursts of expression. These words are free. Unbound by titles, sections, or broader collective theme. Though they are presented as individual pieces, in truth they represent a continual flow: What the tree seeps out. Water drawn from the village well. Their source is singular.

These words are free. Please let them graze and roam and do what wild words do. Please do not feed them lest they grow dependent on human providing. Refrain from seeking to cage them. They cannot be held captive. Do not possess them. They are already possessed. They burn with *ahimsa* fire. These are wild words. Let them possess *you*. Then you will see: Language is an endless place, an open plain, and these words are free.

This is a journey into the interior. That elusive yet decipherable place inside places. The revelation moment inside moments. A sojourn well worth taking, for even the most awesome fields of flowers lose their luster, succumb to seasons, and drop their petals. The Spirit field has no season. If only we can find it and stay there, we are home.

Here is the Tibetan teahouse and all its pristine pleasantries: the gracious host, the hot kettle singing, yak butter and biscuits, the sweet absence of items . . . only windows opening to air so clean and thin we breathe it and are cast into dreaming. Here too is the reckoning found beyond the teahouse. A journey so steep and high and hard that any water we find is frozen into mirrors . . . they block the mountain pass and we have no choice but to gaze into them and see ourselves, so naked of even a scrap of self-deception's cloth.

These words are the imperfect echo of a conversation Eternity has within and all around us. Our lives are the tuning fork. Creation is the eager ear. So here speak stories. Hopefully you will grow quiet inside, so that Silence can speak *your* truth. Then may a song arise in you that is wordless. For when saying becomes being, being is finally said. And when Soul at last says itself, all saying is done.

Come listen to Silence whisper across the red earth of Creation. Come closer . . .

Blinding white snow serves you sunlight
on glinting fields of frozen flakes

your weight crunches this vast array
of snow dishes fallen from sky's pantry
punctuating each of your sluggish steps

your shocked lungs gasp for scant oxygen
in an atmosphere not made for breathing

thoughts race through your teetering mind
like children in the deep woods
deliriously wanting to be lost in a tangent

your body has already decided
that you left your senses back at a
far lower altitude many miles before

it searches for a suitable rock
on which to surrender

you have never been more alive

friend . . . you are a traveler

on failing soles
you have traversed Tibetan valleys in their
lushness of wildflowers—rivers—and pines

you ascended the plateaus
with their assertive winds
until this high alpine of snow leopards
and infrequent shrubs
this secretive life of slopes
and hardness swirling

you have arrived under swelling moon
in a personal season of rebirth and reckoning

so many moons have passed in your life
and yet still your heart thrums daily pleading:
please . . . more moonfuls of light!

you have come from your life of great intentions
your flattening of life's rich circles
into an impotent linearity
occupied with tasks and goals

a linear sleepwalk that completely misses
the luscious river curves and pockets
where treasures are buried in
the damp soil of unmanicured banks

you have come here to Himalaya
with your prized collection of security blankets

each stale with fear and faded of color

over years you took your life of flowers
and fashioned it into a field of worry weeds

now you have come thirsty for soul water
and like a divining rod your body has
pointed you up a mountain . . . this mountain

you can taste the water waiting in this ground
even as the heights steal your sobriety
lifting you into a drunkenness sufficient
to impair your long obsession
with the great ghost *Control*

and so willing one foot and then the next
you climb

you round a path lined in slate rock walls
a gust blasts your frozen face
as if an initiation ritual

for a moment exhaustion threatens
to swallow you whole

the tears clear from your eyes
you regain myopic vision
your entire biology pauses and *you see it:*

there before you at the foot of a high slope
is a teahouse . . . singular and mute

its skin is stone interweaving
roof shingles of tired wood and corrugate

many paths lead here to this buoy-shack
inset on a towering ocean of rock
paths folding always into a single arrival

outside the teahouse
prayer flags ruffle their dowry
in the sharp glacial wind
guardians protecting this place
or perhaps
beacons drawing souls like you near

beside this shelter a moon-faced boy
dark mystic mountain lakes for eyes
draped in maroon and saffron robes
moves a hand across prayer wheels

his hand a flock of cranes
skimming copper water
a prayer for what might swim beneath
the surface of unspeaking day

you approach the teahouse door
numb knuckles knock
your breath dances away as mist

the door of your lifetime opens
teahouse hostess looks out at you

her face is this earth
high and broad
cracked and lined in old roads
curving along steep cliffs and tenuous passes

her cheekbones like land a glacier crossed
pushing its sharp weight and crystal
deep into her rose-sable skin
imbedding all the richness of caravanned life
that a glacier cannot help but to transport

her face is this earth
red and ruddy and personified
frozen and yet still gleaming warmly
with sun's affection

her long black braids are the outcomes
of ancestral looming

generations of thick fingers have oiled
and parted these locks

her own hands might pass for the roots of trees
they have touched just as much life as do roots
drawn heat and stew into a slow parade of bodies

she is this mountain
a mineral summit who rises
and walks each morning
to the faithful bucket and well that she is
to draw herself as water for the old teapot
serving herself stewed with flowers
to what beyond-mountain travelers may come
through the splinter-hided door

your smiling hostess invites you in

now shoeless you seat yourself
on a carpet-covered bench

room's interior warmth
rushes over your life's permafrost
that begins to thaw and drip
and burn in strange relief

wood fire deep in ash utters delicate blue flames
carpets and baskets carouse the floor
sprawled out like lazy animals in sun shafts

His Holiness smiles cherubically at you
from a gold-framed photo on the wall

wildflowers sit in a cup drawing water
a faint memory flutters in you
but does not take flight

hostess offers fat steamed dumplings
and thin pea curry

her own family will eat water
and *sowa tsampa* (oats) that night
yet she is no less pleased to feed you
for a well-attended visitor
leaves karmic blessings in appreciation

she drowns you in endless wooden bowls
of hot salty butter tea
your chapped lips mollify
as your belly bloats

she is very quiet
though when she looks at you
the awakened candles in her eyes
say all the words

you have been missing from your life

floorboards creek
wind whistles through walls
rafters blackened with smoke residue
carry fables told in thin amber lines
etched by the invisible
but only when travelers are not present
to break the code

wooden cups and bowls occupy the pantry
wooden cups for wisdom

teakettle whistles again
hostess brings singing bowls to pitch
metal elements are joined in music

at this high hum a memory wakes in you
of a time before the mountain
when your soul was clean

you taste briefly now in memory
what a pure moment tasted like then

abruptly the memory vanishes
rolled away in fear's avalanche

your attention is back in the teahouse
lungs still grasping at altitude
thighs burning at the miles climbed
hands stinging as they thaw by the fire

you daydream forward to what you desire:
the ample valley beyond this mountain

the absoluteness at the mountain's peak

a courage gathered like firewood
by the accomplishment of summiting
this frozen giant

orchards ripe with validation and affirmation
endless rows of ritual drums
booming their permission
for you to finally *be you*
be you in your heart
be you in your thoughts
be you in your submission to this *mystery*

now you pass out on the teahouse floor
in a light delirium filled with kaleidoscope colors

your spirit has been lifted
in the talons of a Great Eagle
you are a captured prey
swept through far above atmosphere

you are captured . . . by birth's retrieving talons
torn away from solid earth and fluid illusions
hastily introduced to flying—to immersion in air
to helplessness that you never knew
could feel so complete

smoke rises from the teahouse
reaches you above clouds
above your prior blindness

smoke enters you laughing
its voice is the hostess amused by you

smoke of transformation enters you
now you are falling from the top of sky

free and falling
smoke choking off all access to what you
breathed and lived off all your life before

you land softly on a whispering bush
in an endless valley
the acres of ceremonial drums still booming

you walk the furrows pulling up drums
like stalks of sweet corn
they are huskless and roasted
ready and willing to be eaten

you eat drums
you eat drum beats
now their booming permission for you *To Be*
lives inside of you

your own heartbeat
is your self-permission internal
no longer pining for externality

you walk along a stream
to a clearing in the woods

there beneath a tree so tall
that it is a ribbon hanging from sky
or a jewel strung around the neck of universe
beneath this unbelievable waving tree
is the teahouse

you knock on the old door
hostess answers—smiling her face of red earth
laughing her roll of hillside
her two palms with fingers like ten roots
bound as though to be burned like sage
for smoke smudge cleansing
her two palms joined together
in ancestral *Namasté*
—*bowing to the Divine in you*
she offers you all the food she possesses:

bo-jha suma—salty butter tea
that the yak's udder blessed
and some simple biscuits from a brittle package
served on chipped china
that is her proudest possession

you enter—passing under the low doorsill
built for shorter bodies and smaller egos
looking back once over your shoulder
at the bright cascade of Creation
that waits for you

sitting down on a worn blanket
spun on familial loom
you extend your compacted tender body
stretching ecstatically to your full length

warm wooden cup soothes your stiff hands
a tree gave itself for you

you drink—giving yourself in communion
one day maybe you will become a tree

you look through kettle's steam lifting over
abbreviating flames darting in drafts of tango
crescendoing in language of fire

through this steam that bathes open your pores
through this gracious water veil
hostess looks back at you
with her awakened candles for eyes

you see that silently she wears your face
now it dawns in you:
you are hostess

serving yourself
hosting yourself
laughing at your peculiarity and wanderlust

floorboards creek
windows let through just enough of wind's draft
to keep you listening to what this day has scripted

inside your heart
permission beats a steady *BE*

you turn inside out
your spirit becomes form
your form wears spirit for skin

you walk
a body of Light
breathing the mountain
ascending the elevation of air

you have left the teahouse
and found the tea

without a sound
all that marinates in your life
all that Creation imagined of you
in its deepest dreaming
enters you hot and steaming and stewed perfectly
awakens your cells and leads a revolt

you are ready to be served in wooden bowls
and to live a life worthy of stories
to be told by the lips of prayer flags waving
and served along with a proper pot of tea.

One wanderer asks another:

what is your path?

the other replies:

my path has no name
for I do not name it

it is not even a path
for I have always been that which I seek

it is a silence that sings
a morning sun
a mountain spring

it is a giving way of what was never
real enough to be in my way

air itself opens up
what it opens to
is where and what I am.

In a simple moment
a breeze-blessed walk
through a mountain meadow of meditation
you finally decide to Love yourself
and harvest Peace

to seal the promise
you speak these words:

I have decided to become a tree

from this day I will not yearn
but will take my water and sun
as they are given

I will live in unbroken communion
with my sacred soil
holding fast to my roots

I will stand tall and constant
according to my nature
no matter worldly regard for me

I will bow in the wind and be an open heart
for what comes to rest or nest in me

I will not fight the seasons
but drop my leaves in their due time
and grow silent when winter bid me rest

I will acquire age in annual rings that
display my gaining texture
and I will not shame

I will shade the weary and hold up the weak

I will host an audience of cicadas
and let them speak

I will not waver before opinion
or question my peculiar bloom

self-consciousness will not know me
for I will be plunged in currents of being
and will bear no doubt within

I will not fear
I will be hostage to true Love

birthing faithful fruit
from the bright womb of sanctuary

my wounds will heal into gnarly knots
of morph and revelation

sky will bless my nakedness
with the elements that it chooses
and I will seek no shelter

I will not forget my ancestors
assault my neighbors
or offer an offending tongue

I will whistle inside gusts
laugh by way of children
roam richly in the storm

I will cry my sap freely
and wear my bark with tenderness

when young Love carves its dreams
into my giving side
I will abide

I will grow wherever my seed is sprung
and let my story beautify me

I will unsheathe my fragrance
and release my saplings to their own rendition
my branches never getting in the way

I will not begrudge the saws and axes
nor gnaw against myself

when the spiteful ones come to spite me
I will disappear into Love and not be touched

I will carry my foliage modestly
and endure the pride of creatures

in all the noise and noxious grinding
I will remain silent and smiling
my cadence steady and yet not saddled
throwing any harness
I will not be addled

I will be Peace
I will be Love
I will be in the chaos . . . still
and by the moment
as others trade their souls
for carnival attractions
I will be still . . . a tree.

In this new light
silence dreams of running free again

dreams of itself as a sugar cane stalk
weeping its Love in clear drops
down the tender jade shaft

a brook pouts
wanting more sun
which is denied in palms of shadow

air performs against a fallen
form of wood
its encore is unseen

it dances nonetheless
and summons brio
to sing a high-pitched note
its tongue a throttling of leaves

in this new light
beggars gain closer to the throne
their rags glint in the eyes of
children whose lesser obstruction
allows them to discern
royal robes beneath the squalor

in this new light
suffering's point begins to summarize

despair heaps against the inner walls
of the human heart

microscopic fissures spread from chambers
out into arterial canyons

our dam of social delusion shows its
age against the strain

insects—animals—and perforated souls
sense the impending flood
and together take to the sky
in flocks of story

they meet in the meadow
between moon and sun

from that patch of dewy revelation
they sing praise and the sky
falls down in rain
where it forms a brave torrent
across our arid earth

some of us toe the water

some leap in and are carried
lost and found
in this new light.

A young monk goes walking
with his teacher along the ocean shore

pupil decides to refresh himself
takes off his clothes
jumps into the cooling sea

this water is freezing! he shrieks

his teacher
palms clasped
smiles and says:

stop criticizing the water

the young monk is puzzled:
what do you mean?

teacher responds:
it is you who are freezing
the water feels just fine with itself
our reaction to the world tells us
more about our self
than about the world to which we react

all judgments are relative to the one
who is judging

all reactions tell a story
about the one who is reacting

life's moments are for teaching
and for learning
both of which depend on whether
we swing the looking glass
in the right direction

now come get dressed

you may be freezing
but you are giving the ocean a fever!

The young monk
fearing his mortality
seeks comfort from his teacher
a wise word to alleviate his fear

teacher obliges:

Do not be afraid of dying
while you are alive

be afraid of living
while you are dead

every soul who has ever lived
has died

not every soul who has died
has lived

there is a choice in this
deep in fiber of the flesh
of the seed of the moment
potential lies waiting
its latency the force
of a mountainside of lambs
yearning for the teat

sunrise is a straining beacon
caged below ground by your
stilted approximation of joy

take an axe to the shell
decimate your prison

stop looking for the train to arrive
it has always been here

now it is leaving
say your goodbyes to mediocrity
and attachments

get to know the sensation of
nothingness beneath your feet

learn the maiden name of *Freedom*
be a naked bird never intending to land.

Can your soul come out and play?

all the others have been grounded
by their fearful parents

instead of enjoying this sweet twilight
walls and doors close in on them

a slight rain is falling
can your soul come out and taste it?

I know of a secret river in the woods
we can find pieces of bark
sail them like ships down the current
skip stones until our arms fall off

my dear friend Voci told me of a field
where laughter grows like fat cornstalks

we could go there and race down
the saffron colored rows
brushing the stalks into hilarity

we could stay out all night and
drink milk from the half moon's bowl

bats dart in the dark sky ocean
we could hitch a ride on one
and fall into the Divine heart

wouldn't that be something?

look—I am not asking for too much am I?
just that you take off that awful coat
you have been wearing all your life
it smells of joy denied
as though weevils crawled into
its pockets and died

Great Spirit has laid down
this glorious meal of endless courses
it is steaming on the old oak table

come and eat with me
we won't even have to do the dishes
this meal comes magically into the mouth
needs no serving bowl

you eat a bite and the food replaces itself

even if your appetite were that
of a hundred growing children
you could not overtake this meal

all-you-can-eat is not just a slogan
it is an invitation from Paradise
beckoning us across the bridge
that joins our unfulfilling life
to the grand celebration taking place
beyond the curtain mundane

I know you have been grounded
but can't you sit down
and have a conversation
with your fearful parents?

after all we aren't talking about
the parents who raised you

we're talking about the parents
you have become to your self

you've even given them names
one you have named *Excuse*
the other you call *Responsibility*

I say become an orphan
run away!

you won't need a knapsack
or any clothes

this running requires only nakedness
plus the ability to tear out your heart
from the clenched cage of your suffering

we won't be going very far
yet we'll travel farther than you can imagine

this new place
where our souls will play
is the beach that a million suns visit
to bathe in the Great ocean
and lay out on the Sacred sand

sunlight goes there to get a tan

you won't believe the brilliance
all the shadows you have known
will evaporate in that smiling chaos

come on now
no more excuses—reasons—responsibilities
ahhh . . . there . . .
I feel you moving

see!
your soul wants to come out and play!

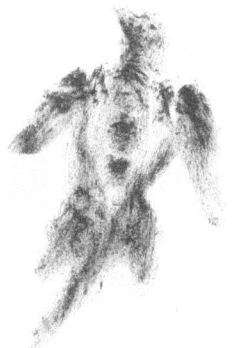

A bright sparrow brings you seeds of joy

first you hear the song of melody
the sweet chirping framed in sunlight

then you abandon your mind of daily logic
and enter an amphitheatre of awakening

in this state finally you hear the lyric
that your own heart writes in plaintive patience:

Come and live with me in this present
your old house does not suit you

its air is sad and heavy
yet you keep inhabiting it as if
it is your Lover

it is not your Lover
it is a cruelness taunting you

it was built for a moment
that has long since passed

you are stuffing yourself into pants
that you have far outgrown
get naked and breathe again

come live with me in this present
our house together will have fresh water
and sunlight pouring through wide windows

there will be a place for you to lie on the floor
in the brightness and be drowsy

silence will be your music
a nice breeze will be your cup of tea

there will be laughter
and outside children stirring up the leaves

here
take my hand
you do not have far to go
this road has no actual distance
it is a matter of release

brush is scattered on your forest floor
waiting for you to set it afire
such dying brings new life

your mind is the match
close your eyes
smile
breathe free
and strike your Peace.

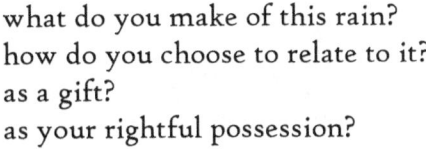

Y ou are walking in a cauldron of desert

suddenly sweet rain cascades over you
blessing your skin
pooling in your pores
relieving your fear of imminent death

what do you make of this rain?
how do you choose to relate to it?
as a gift?
as your rightful possession?

do you cherish each drop
or do you begin to fantasize about
bottling this heavenly water
stocking as much as possible for yourself
and selling the rest on the market to others
just as desperate as you?

and what if sweet rain comes to you as a person?
what will you make of this person
who cools your boiling chaos
and touches open the valve of your reprieve?

will you try to bottle this person-water
or will you stand mouth and soul agape
in this wondrous rain
receiving what it brings

performing the joy of two living things
who come together?

sweet rain has a source which is sky
it comes therefore from everywhere
is meant to fall freely
intended to cycle through earth and elements
bound not by our desire or attachments
but moved by Love's essential enormity.

With each breath
we recreate the world

a canvas for our sacred
walk through life

our clouds of Love and compassion
drawn from boundless waters
to blanket sky

and rain down on earth
the beauty of being.

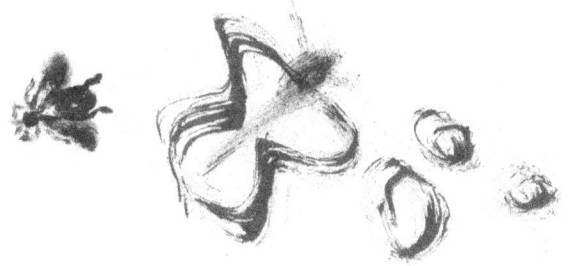

Catching butterflies is not like
catching fireflies
butter is not fire
day makes butterflies more beautiful
night treats fireflies the same

in whose light or blackness
does your best beauty show itself?

all essence is relative to what we hold essential

why do so many of us allow geysers of ugliness
to gush from our pores so often so easily
while some plug those malice-holes
with Love-caulking they mix
in the mortar of their hearts?

say the thing you always wanted to say
say it to the one whose beauty
takes your breath away
so that she does
take your breath away

this act of saying
would bring it back

your breath

touch beauty when you see it
not so as to smudge or desecrate it
touch so that it becomes more beautiful

do you know this skill?

once you do the world is yours
and you should have no reason
to be a destroyer

silence is an opening unto the self
do not belittle its possibilities

rain does not fall
it races toward that which
would transform it

when water touches a thing
water is born again

we might try this behavior
moving with secret determination
toward that which will shuffle
our rigid habits into a fine silt
that is not so afraid of being poured

if you keep giving me moments
I will keep cooking this stew

if you insist on puckering your lips
to the serving spoon
I won't stop finding new ways
to get the soup inside your soul

if you believe the gossip of night birds
you would think the clanging
of iron in the wind was the mating call
of some strange species

it is not

what noise you hear at this midnight
is the conversation day makes while sleeping

it is planning itself
pay close attention

wind chimes are not for our sake
they are the tools of impending moments
music meant for Love's foreplay
not for the vacancy of idle hearts

chew on this licorice root for a moment
your lungs will open up and give you
a chance to breathe in something useful

when you spit out the juices on the ground
a crooked sprout will emerge
to show you the direction of your life's leaning
so you can *straighten up*

time remains as long as breath is with you
to chart a course away from the vortex
in which you lose yourself
onto a path that at least is lined
with trees and dreams

some say your persona is best served
on fine china from the special pantry

others say why not use the paper plates
the juices will run and stain the carpet
either way

no use pretending the plate itself
is something special
or capable of raising the value
of what gets served

serve the thing
the quicker the better
get it out and into their hands

heavenly morsels cannot act out
their heavenliness until they are
being swallowed

this is true also for the gifts
we have to offer

such as Love.

Remember when we were walking
through silent woods

you shouted

no reason except that you feared
the absence of your own voice

I suppose you thought you were
being swallowed

mistaking sound for soul does this
to a person

when we believe that two souls walking
need noise to celebrate their togetherness

this is like pouring honey
between the piano keys

what we pour is sweet to our tongue
but to the keys it is death

sweet or sour means nothing
within the bouquet of circumstance

you poured honey
the keys still play
but the sound is slow
and works harder than it should
in order to be born

wonderfully though these same woods
offer us a serendipitous revival

a hollowed out knotting low near the base
of an old tree that groans in wind
can serve as an aperture through which to look
and see ourselves as we were meant to be

bend low sweet one and look through
the eyepiece crafted by time working with wood

through the space left by what is missing
from the old knot just above the floor of leaves
see what can be present in our intimacy:

a fairytale of harmony
the only thing impeding its birth into reality
the noise we churn out in fear

grow silent dear
and there in those quiet woods
dropping the role play of relationship
let us gather scattered branches
and build the one thing
that warms all souls to speak:

union fire that sears True Love
into Lovers who want only to be true.

Peace is not a desire

it is an excavation

stop looking for more words
dear friend
start digging

this poem is over!

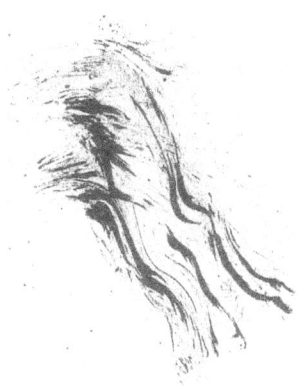

You are blessed
and life is blessed by you

you are Loving life
and life is Loving you

there is no Great Stream running
into a smaller stream

there is only one Great Stream

you are That
and It is you

you are not just a cup
rendered passive to receive

you are the pourer of the wine
and the wine itself

you are the grapes that
sacrificed themselves

you are sacrifice's leap

you are the sweetness that
bathes inside the wine

you are the bathing

this is not poetry
but the source of poetry
the vineyard that ends
in barrels and feasts

this is not illusion but union
no mirrors are needed to bend this light.

Today Voci and I
are in the garden
blessed with sun and breeze
that cools our skin

maple roots crawl from soil
and curl up beside us
—eager children who know poetry
is flowing here

Voci is smiling
which is like saying the world is happy

Voci drops a weathered hand
and scatters grains of air onto
azaleas—petunias—buttercups

this sacrament brings garden into
a naked blush

we are swirling together away
into the chasm of ages

we have forever to tell each other stories

this place is not kin to time or endings
human calipers cannot measure this

a foolish stanza from me
and Voci is laughing
which is like saying all earthquakes
have awakened at once

Voci's legs are crossed
my heart is open

Voci's heart is failing slowly
but successfully
I have long ago crossed over
to the shore of peace in this regard

yellow jackets pounce on each other in mid air
something new will come of this tumbling

we smell clover—mint—and wild onion
and realize such is life

another chamber yields its holdings
further within my bleating soul
a sweet spring laced with bitter root
emerges lacey and silver from my tongue
a poem has been born and become
water flowing without a soil bed

breeze is enough to carry poem
to Voci waiting
soon Voci is coated in ecstasy
legs aquiver like a colt

which is like saying the universe
has caught a splendid fever

we are home.

Two go walking

a rock is kicked

earth responds:

Do not be so hard on that rock
it was not always so cold and stony

not long ago it was sand
before that soil
even further back it was a yellow flower

you would have kissed it then and felt
it soften to your lips

you would have called it Beauty

pick up the rock
kiss it deeply
you may be surprised to feel an entire
meadow against your mouth

looks can be deceiving
existence moves to an inspired choreography
creation crosses paths with itself endlessly

in every moment God watches to see
if we recognize ourselves in each other

the trickery is in the clothes we wear

now
do you truly see the rock?
yes she was once something you could Love

kiss her.

We stand in a river
dying of thirst for Love

what we seek is all around us
yearning for our invitation

we could drown so sweetly
if only we learned to recognize
the many faces of our Beloved.

A farmer wants the market vendor
to place *him* on a proper scale
so the vendor can finally
see the farmer's true value:

My barley is equal to that man's wheat

the molecules choose another design
to become you apart from me

but they are the same matter
in the starfish as in the redwood tree

you pretend canyons separate our natures
and yet the only canyon between us
is the behemoth of your imagination

we are the same stream
my water your water what does it matter?
they mix themselves a billion times for
each stretch of the river that binds us

we disappear into one another
so rapidly as we flow
that the current grows giddy

we are actors wearing each other's robe
thinking it to be our own exclusive garment

what foolish *nonseers*

even the spider knows tomorrow
it will be the fly.

Has the camel no right to purr
or the sea bass to bark?

all variation of Being is sewn
into the entire inventory

the sewing occurred at dusk
in the half-light of day and night turning

we cannot see the thread
and so we say:
that doll can speak
and that one can sing
all that one does is cry

we forget the Manufacturer
knows all the tricks for inserting magic
into the whole production line

every doll can do *all things*

each new life from tree to us to stone
carries its brethren within its nature

stop doing for a moment
just *be* and you will hear
the silent chorus singing:
I am that too.

Sunlight opens the flower
of the human heart

be the sun!

A compassionate one tosses fitfully in bed
in the deepest hour of night

the words pour forth from a bruised heart
longing to be heard
by a companion in the silence:

They have said I am a prophet

I am but a poor jagged rock
faithfully washed over by God
Grace brings out whatever beauty
I might claim

I am the shrill whistle made bearable
by Creation's gracious cloaking breath
the ungainly stride
steadied by unseen Hands

look for me in mud's bottom
this is how far I fall from Grace
and yet I am chosen to spread
some manner of goodness
through my living

how undeserving am I?

too many times my tongue
has blistered souls

too often my touch
has desecrated what should
have been honored

my heart has conspired
manipulation and control

my mind has joined the conspiracy

I have lost myself more times
than the moments of my life
for in each moment
I have lost myself in multitude

I am a mule pulling a nonexistent carriage

what I have cared for is no more than vapors
while What cares for me goes denied
in my vacant breast

this is neither despair nor darkness
rather the opposite—I am ecstatically broken
on the hard rocks of my imperfection
and this earnest spilling
is the beauty of my dissolution

Glory has lit my lamp
my heart is afire and joy frosts my totality

now I know that even my failing
can be used for Beauty
by the Greatness
we only think we know.

Excuse me

that grass was meditating
before you sat on it.

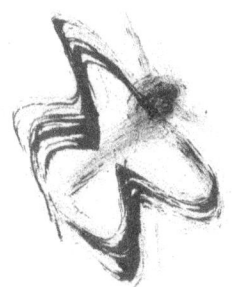

Sometimes our fears
make monsters out of butterflies

practice your relationship with Creation

using that newfound source of power
vanquish the monsters
and let butterflies come to stay.

A tree grows for 40 years

one day a flock of blackbirds
arrives through bright sky and settles
on its highest sun-sparkling branches
a sweet moment of union

this is what it means to be patient

purpose arrives when it will

in the meantime
let us grow into it.

Decibels wave in desert silence
wooden wind chimes
aloft in my wilderness

sky lifts its curtain
reveals its dance of hawk and cloud
passing their pantomime shadows
over granite architecture left by time

on desert floor a tiny meadow
of butter-yellow and pale lavender flower faces
and she kneels down to inhale their graces

hollow knocking places on curvature of stone
cathedral walls
earthen animals in granular repose

belly of sunlight dropped into creased lap
of this Grand creation

wind translated
into a thousand tongues
one for each stiff afro of Joshua tree

a lone purple flower strung in bells
along a stubborn stem

clandestine operation of Herculean ants
lime fungal colonies creeping
in pockets of shade on skin of stones

melancholy spilled over sacred metropolis
echoing back to that singular spring of origin

sewing needles growing graciously
from huddled cacti pitched in spiny reverie
pin cushion for so many Native hands

portraiture of faces in granule relief
constant unseen turning chronic and brief

bulbous fruit crowning motley trees
teal reptile gathering last fruit of sun
beetles in the branches
tiny ants perched on tiny bud

skeletal remains of a shrubbish flower
splayed in white grey webbing

Joshuas wearing delicate white hair
of old men and women
descending decay's staircase
back into earth
into cool reunion

yucca swords en guarde
and peeling at the edge

pancake stacks and
dinosaur vertebrae
book cases and windows
all forms revealed in rock
a population of voyeurs
and agate sentries

sand grains
offspring of rain—rock—wind
of biting cold and colossal heat

ponderous gusting lung of valley
mountain range's abject exception
earth's concave iteration
grand cotillion in the canyon
capstone proud of bonnet

bilious breeze
capitulating limbs of trees
arboreal ashes
beards of sharp bark
plummeting necklines of horizon
staircases—zippers—spines sewn in stone
outback of parody and effigy

dry decanter of trunks deposed and standing
proud pillars stubborn for the stage

slabs of boulder shorn and cantilevered
against their cousins

cantankerous weeds calmed
at the foot of proud pavilions

heirlooms of polished mineral
painted walls
evidence of waterfalls

private chambers deep in the rock
lyric pools and shafts of light
baths of stone erosion
epiphanies of outline on plains of vastness

intrepid birthing
epidemic emergence
slow and glacial only to the myopic eye
of relativity

and at night . . .
obsidian

indigo
silhouette

surrender to a ceiling reinvented
a supreme blackness perforated
in scattered bursts of distal flame

this place
this brevity of expression
languorous tide
so flush with life
so absent of obvious water

so aching a monument
to Creation's aftermath and foreplay

landscape of dreams
themselves dreaming.

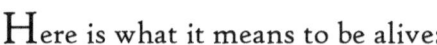

Here is what it means to be alive:

If you have it—give it

if you are water
do what water does when the glass is full
and someone wants a drink

do not pretend to be sand—unable to help
just so you can excuse
the hoarding of your wealth

be what you are—give what you have

and here is a secret: give it all

the volume of your true wealth has no limit
it does not reside in a vault of brick or stone
has no walls—floor—ceiling to contain it

it sits in a shell-less gourd and replaces itself
tenfold each time it pours out

shatter your imagined container
and find out what true richness is

the form we obsess over
is dung rolled by a beetle
leave that to the beetle!

loosen your purse
see it filled with endless sun
and burst into a thousand purses

if you are water
do what water does

flow and end another's thirst.

Self:

That part of the universe possessing
a particular density of vibration
that a person comes to claim as being
who she is

a cloud we believe is our home
a patch of sand on the dunes that
we stake as ours just before the wind arrives

a membrane around our wetness
that prevents us from joining the ocean

the shadow we inhabit
in the persistent dream
in which the world is split
and everything exists in pieces

a particle of existence
that tends to feel it is better or worse
than all the rest but which has trouble
just being a part of the rest

the idea we possess
that never lets us rest

the profound ladder we climb
skin we shed
eggshell we escape
veil we dispense
idea we renovate
to find our way back to selflessness.

A willowy silent servant
performs nightly ritual
of meditation by the river...

by the river
obsidian movement in moonlight
glistening a language
that washes the rocks
brushes harried nerves
strung inside this human visitor

stroking softly human tension
into releasing itself
a breeze into water

by the river
bathing in lunar shower
bathing in dissolution
in the damp soil of riverbank

swaying in a hammock of breeze
fastened to pithy stars
threading peace through the
needle eye of emptiness

the focused oblivion
shedding notions
shedding check points and scripts
leaving these dead cells
to burn away on the boiling rocks
of brilliant nothingness

nocturnal life breathes a sound of river

diurnal stirring lies down to sleep
serenaded by fluid gush of current
and this soul by the river
forgetting
looking at itself looking
seeing itself seeing itself

sky arcs in immeasurable depth
its blackness pouring . . . pouring
moon peers
stars scamper
hours grow inert
day pours out from this
glorious dark breast
evaporates in the black
dissipates in purification

nascent fertility
waking in the black

suspended soil aerated . . . receiving
diluting into this passage of pristine darkness
this wet coursing
beside the river
this dry aproning of tears
arid obstinacy refusing itself
tumbling through its iterations
incapable of being touched
in the same place again
for it is wondrously placeless

a beacon saying
come be this too
stars will fall into you
all that lives will drink from you
and you will not want

for want requires form
and you will be acutely emancipated
from that tortuous containment

you will be exhalation—exhaler—exhaled

all of this is why these many occasions
this dutiful returning to the river
in the shade light of night

this doing nothingness
this departure from identity
long immediate brevity un-urgent
languorous self-watching of
this watcher watching
until all doing closes its flower
and sleeps into waking

where night winks
against the river
that in its knowing flows.

A particular conversation occurs
inside of air undisturbed by our spoken words

absent that turbulence of talk
Truth comes rushing in

one moment we are throttling our vocabulary
doing a poor imitation of God's omniscience

the next moment we are finally mute and opened

Creation in us grasps this opening and cries out
with the pristine clarity of a temple bell

two magnets face-to-face
with their poles aligned in complement
rush to each other like aching Lovers

our souls and Sacredness run toward each other
with the same profound urgency

but only when our poles are aligned in harmony

sunlight seeks the heart of rose
but she must open to be fully blessed
for a rose exposed receives the bounty
of what sun already knows

our souls and Sacredness can be such Lovers

words or no words
openness is the vital pose
and quietude that arrangement.

In the soft nook of an old tree
on a canyon side painted in night
a luminescent beating heart
calls out to a known soul
on the canyon's far side:

Would you have drawn your arrow
and sent its force into my place of origin
had you known a spring of wanting
would burst forth into a geyser?

known soul answers:

Yes
for I am nothing
but that which goes
where wanting grows

I am that swollen plum
gathering my sugar and flesh
preparing to be dearly eaten

I am dying to be devoured
in the collective aching heart

I am suffrage on the lip

I am called out of the chasm
to return to the chasm
with bits of light
and frayed notes
from a song

I have come for those
who bleed in the dire dust

I am a bee driven mad
by the sweet pollen
of joy and laughter

I am dew dropped by sky
into the tearful buttercup heart
of the passionate ones

I am sky
pouring out over itself

earth running over its earth

I cannot stop this weeping
which is my own weeping
left in washed out gullies
in villages of despair
to mark faces in salt
so this Love can find them

I have a kite string tied to joy's updraft
I will not let go

when the fearsome beast
roars in the apogee of our primal fear
I will kneel to stroke its broad sternum
and offer my head to its daggered jaws
if that be my fate

I am drawn to wanting
that phosphorescent tidal pool
from which I first emerged
slick and sniffing air
when dawns had yet no light

this stretched skin
I shred in every moment
is the drumhead handed down
by the ones who sing in darkness
and hew light from charcoaled walls of cave

they who with sharp bleached bone
spill their hearts at the river
feeding the valley their red romance
of Lovingness

they who see the mist
inside the minutiae seen by solemn seers

they who cover their faces
in old mud and dance in the cold current
until new corn grows

they have given me this skin
that taunts me in its echo
and leaves from me daily
aloft in tattered uprisings

this heart within is a sounding bell
only the deepest soulful yearning
in this world can make it tremble

and when it moves
its only voice is an absolute elation
destined for those fields of wanting
brushed by sky beneath sky
in their unattended serendipity.

A bright lotus grows brighter

moon's glance causes this delight

mimic the moon.

Wishing for a blank white page of soul
on which to inscribe clarity

this is a daily task
a gathering of stream water
at its cleanest point

bearing the load in trembling arms
of panicking muscle

trudging up mud-anointed mountain paths
finally boiling the kettleful on the fire

this is a wildfire of silence
chasing away the woods creatures
that are busyness and chatter

this is stillness on its knees remembering
the birth of land and cooling of sea

a black bird comes down
from the ceiling of sky
fanning malcontents in the blazing brightness
of what it has seen

what if the last increment of fear
could be flushed from our fibers?

it can

but there is a requirement:
we must be willing to ascend into foolishness
—that transformed state of leaving the trough
to feed from the higher pasture

a driver commands a horse and carriage
along a perilous mountainside road

nervous and blind we assume he must
tighten his rein-grip to survive

instead he lets go
everything plunges into the abyss:
horses—carriage—driver

nervous and blind we exclaim in horror:
the driver must be mad!

could we but see we would celebrate
for the abyss is no death trap
it is the deep pool of serenity

this dream is not what it seems
carriage is a comfortable habit
horses are true soul power
bridled by our desire to control
the reins are fear
and the driver is not going anywhere
on the mountainside except in circles

until he lets go

we think the road to be safety
but it is our prison of suffering

only by giving up all that we
believe keeps us safe and sane
can we possibly plunge into the place
of no harm and no insanity

the empty place that at first feels to us
as though we are falling
with nothing solid beneath our feet

this initial rush of falling
is in fact reunion with the wordless place
that we come from and are

we must be the driver
choosing being over doing
so that being can show us how
to truly do what we came here for

which is to *Be.*

If there is sun
in your sky today
cherish it

if there is not
imagine your gratitude
when it shall return again.

A bow to Basho...

single plum blossom
dancing on unseen stage of sky
is enough.

A branch drops to ground
from a tall tree
homecoming.

A bird pale-yellow in sun
skims lake's unhurried surface
both flight and stillness reflected.

Woodpecker's habit sounds
from a clear distance
echo joins chorus of woods.

Sunlight turns simple leaf
into magical flag of color
joy does the same to quietude.

Dragonflies chase each other
across lake's mirror
no one ever wins.

Two nights ago full moon
behind clouds behind treetops
still shining through.

On a bench
under stand of shade trees
perfect warmth.

Water's reflection ripples across
sunlit leaves and pines
remembering ocean tides.

Squirrel leaps high over tall
shocks of grass and again
agile forager.

Squirrel now high up
a towering tree
new perspective.

Scenes like this
lake and sky and song of trees
what would Basho have written?

How many days in the whispering cave
seeking the inner place
would it take before aloneness
became a festival of revelation?

how many prayers before the moss
grows a language for saying things
potent enough to wake our languor?

what depth the cavern river
before light cannot breach its belly?

what lives within the deeps
illuminated not by sun?

how vast the music of the hollow's
endless chambers?

how pure the tones of sequestered moments
strung across the heart
an heirloom bright and rosy?

and the bath in the limestone circle
sulfurous vapors tickling up the stalagmites'
slick and oozing slopes

sour emanation whose only want
is to go on curling

the stacked stones at the wall's foot
gray and cadenced against themselves
marking prior presence
yearning for those to come

bright wind at the mouth
beckoning bravely
for who knows what might
come answering from the dark

and still the secluded body
drinking light into its heart
rubbing fingers against smoothened stones

a mutual massage

kneeling between hard places
leaning on the strong tree of emptiness

dozing off behind vanguard of pines
to serenade of breeze along chosen crevasse
away from a world of quailing

fattening on the fruit inside the moment
grain swelling on the loom of dreaming

in the cave
that womb of a possible inner place
contracting at the call of moon.

A storyteller of caramel skin
and lightning white hair
walked up upon a wilted man
one day on the road of life

the man knelt at the roadside
lips cracked and parched
searching the bushes for berries or blossoms
anything to slake his arid body of its dry agony

the man looked up at the storyteller
her own lips full and healthy
no trace of distress upon her aged face

he asked:
how long have you been walking this road?

Storyteller answered:
near to forever—far as I can tell

this troubled the man:
how is it possible that you can walk this road
for so long and not be close to death
what with this interminable heat?

this is when Storyteller
picked up her walking stick
sat down beside the man and commenced

to share herself for a spell

she answered:

I drink waterfalls of this world
from tall glasses of imagination

quench my thirst for Truth by pouring the
universe down my throat

this is how one day I found the Sacred
within the skin of living

what's this?
the sacred skinning?
the man queried

no child
the Sacred within the skin of living
Storyteller corrected him
continuing on:

the skin of living speaks to you and says
lick your wounds

the Sacred says praise your wounds
for they have opened you
the pain you feel is the doorstep
to the rest of you
the all of you that hovers a cloud
within and around you
even as you purse your lips in fright
and try to blow that cloud away

the skin of living says praise your wisdom

the Sacred says be shy of your wisdom
for it is merely the bud before the blossom
the tart green promise that becomes
the sweetened fruit

true wisdom is the tunnel whose entrance
you have just barely breached
and all around is earth that may fall down
upon you the moment you celebrate yourself
too loudly

the skin of living says fight who hurts you

the Sacred says Love who hurts you
for unbeknownst to them
they have made you rich of ways
to progress your self

the broken bone healed is stronger than before
hurt precedes strengthening like life lived
that becomes the lore

the skin of life says elude the odd of character

the Sacred says take the odd in arm and dance
for their strange song will lead you to places
your own music has not before

the skin of life says cower in the rain
seek shelter in the sun
don't walk when you can run

the Sacred says open your mouth to the sky
and drink the rain's water
swim in the light of sun
and for Goodness sake walk precisely
because you can run

can do and *should do* are not Lovers but
temptation's pairing whispered in covert breath

the skin of life is composed of fat
you intend to use for a hibernation
that never comes

you feel it protects you
though it encases you
restrains you
laughs at the stifled surges of your growth

even snakes walk tall enough to know
when to shed their outer to release their inner
so cycle can begin again

Storyteller paused
for she was near to through

she said:

you and I have been walking the same road

to you the road has been hot and blistering

for me the same road has been
cool and comfortable

again I say
I drink waterfalls of this world
from tall glasses of imagination
quench my thirst for Truth
by pouring the universe down my throat

but you
your suffocating heat is self-generated

your Sacred surges
bursting to get out
so Truth can get on in

my child
your season whispers to you this:

it is time to shed your skin
and surrender to the bliss.

If I have said this poem before
I say it now again—consumed

it will not go away
this burning exhortation
this willow stripped
and bleeding its glass fluidity
into my sonorous vesicle of innerness

have you seen the inferno
of a forest on fire while standing

close enough to feel the alchemy
of your own melting?

such is my heart against
the towering wave of this poem
this poem charging its heat and potency
into the origin of my universe
stampeding its brilliance
across my contentment
thundering its earth
into my earth
upheaving soil plates
grown to dust
into airborne thistles
of new serration
and reckoning
all within
my heart
my mind
my cloth
I wave
inside
ideas

have you seen the last
snorting of the bison
before it buries you
under its hooves
beneath its brawn
drawn from castles
of muscle and sinew
its weight of herbivorous
might and singularity
stamping your carnivorous

smallness down into the dark
rampant mud of the moat?

what did your last breath
taste like?

whose face came glimmering
into your mind just before
you drew blank and black
descending away from
all this light
all this world of things
you thought you knew
thought you needed
thought you Loved

then the fitful burst back up
through the aqueous surface
your lungs now novas tearing
for the slightest breath
shredding their sacs
sacrificing continuity
for a desperate kiss of air

and you alive again
this time truly living
swimming through swamp and limerick
for the shore
for the sand and soil that you—having changed
will never step upon again so heavily
for your feet are gone
departed with your magma of fear
and your phlegm of blindness

instead of feet
you are now endowed with
appendages that can only
be described as that which
is used for flying

your heart is helium
your blood flash distilled from viscous syrup
to diaphanous mist

your mind killed of its rampaging ideologies
you are a cane of sugar
your stalk is cut and crying
your Love pours out
you cannot stop
and that is why

you are free.

In the silence that dawns
when silence itself grows mute
in that silence
let this torch of Love find you
and burn away all that binds you
to the bloated carcass of identity

become tinder for Love-fire
translucent language escaped of its skin
pasture just beyond the conceivable

verdant valley beneath Asiatic eye
black cascade
surrender's sigh

yourself seeing yourself lifted
formless
flying away on thermal rivers

come back to your garden
by letting go of its iron gates
and stone wall periphery

let your lust lurch into the sunlight
and vanish in that epiphany

learn the language of trees

fall in Love with your nonhuman admirers
they will hold you closer than
any two arms or cloistered heart

polish the crystal eye of true seeing
insert its orb into your ocularity

go stumbling in the dark until
your soul adjusts to seeing what
lives in shadows

set down your armament
pick up the signs that insecurity
drops all around you

fashion those illusions into
a bouquet of iris
return it in Love
to the ones who dropped their despair
in usual costumes at your feet

die farther
splice your fear and hope
climb that enigmatic rope above clouds
above atmospheres
reach strata ultimo
blister
burst
disperse
fall down in rain on all of this
in silence

in silence give birth
to something worthy of sound.

We are a drunken spider
caught in a web of words it has itself woven

we see the light
but as we move toward it we are snared
in words we have chosen to define the light

we sense the light but cannot locate it
in the very same morass of words
we have been taught to explain the light

we cannot help but weave a garment of words
as impulse of our existence

we are spiders
born to weave words
to expel silken stories from our soul
and frame this life in meaning

we fall into words
as mastodon falls into mud pit

we cage ourselves in words
just as convict merges fearfully
into the consistent walls of his cell
eventually abstaining from freedom
even when given the choice to leave his prison

we are thirsty for the assuring potion of certainty
so we drink our words
our world of words
ravenous and desperate
until—inebriated on the fermentation
of words corked and kegged
bottled and bound
we pass out into the oblivion of those
who have forgotten that words
are not the Truth
but the window through which
we may behold Truth

and that to reach Truth and bathe in its light
we must leave the very dwelling we erected
to locate Truth in the first place

we must leave that dwelling and muster
the courage to go naked into the desert
where Truth hums such a magnificent reverberation
it can never be saddled in word

and so we toil
our limbs caught in the web adhesive
our great irony spilling before us by the moment:

gifted with words to cast light on our meaning
those same word-web strands are also a tar pit
that if we are not mindful—heartful—free
will claim us
to be gazed upon by future tourists
our bones pitched askew in the mire
a species extinct because it could not resist
the rich seduction
the persistent deceit of words as Truth itself

we bring this web into the world
its tensile structure lifting us closer into the light
and by breath of wind also casting us
in collective drift away from the light

the blessing is this:
we can sober through practice
a practice of endless means that reminds us
of the true purpose of the web:
as rampart to the light

and of the true nature of the web:
not as Truth itself but as drumbeat of Truth

we are as that which is cold
toward what is warm

we are created to be drawn toward the flame

our words can carry us a piece of the way

in the end—to reside in Truth
we must take the fatal step in faith
and slough our membrane of word and idea

and facing that awesome moment
of absolute nudity
as Divinity sheers our constructs
and floods our soul
we die beautifully into the light
born at last into the free sky
of illuminated life.

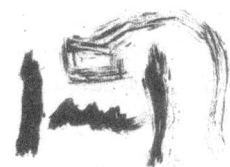

Endless pilgrimages to sit at the foot
of this hermit they call holy

upon arrival they are greeted
with a leaf-full of cold well water
and this quiet murmur:

All the words I have ever written
are nonsense

these present words:
nonsense

I am saying
do not get caught in the ocean my friend

swim in it and move on
for land offers other revelation water

lilac is a wonderful blossom
to smell and swoon beside
but you cannot stay there forever sniffing
you must live your life—keep moving

words and notions are Venus Flytraps
careful how you linger over them
you may soon be trapped inside
devoured in the voraciousness
of your proud convictions

so fall into these words
but do not be possessed

can you catch my drift
while letting it go?

this is the trick:
to touch everything
and hold nothing

to fall into the abyssal vat of Love
and continue drowning even after
you have drowned.

Sometimes she finds a moment
to remember her True path
telling herself:

I braise a path through desert at dawn
my visible breath leaving me
to reunion with light clouds tracking
still dark ceiling of the world

I braise a path with my dream wealth
a treasure of desires and fears
that I have hosted on the long trail
of my generations

my expelled air grows invisible
as candle climbs the sky
spreading its warm quilt over chilled sandstone
queuing night predators to their diurnal sleep

I set my feet step by step on earth
like dry leaves falling

gentle as my distant grandmother taught me

I walk with the softness of quails
my heart pulsing with the stealth
of wolves as I stalk my peace

my solitude a loud fragment
of this canyon's silence

echoing of intimacy with
more verdant domains

my intent heavy and stubborn
a whole herd of bison given to the graze

my full lips crack in the aridity
as does the ground I touch
its brocade of breaks bearing crevasse shelter
for what lives in that penetrating shade

my soul's compass set for a cave
I have never managed to make residence
though I have tasted fleetingly
its calm and felicity inside my heart

the story of my ancestors is carved
on the cave's obsidian walls

their shapes and shadows
are trying to tell me
who I am

I know enough to know
I am not the elk
and at least must be the river

the rest of me is answered inside
this vacuous mouth of earth

all my life of days brings me to this desert
vast extremity conspiring me along my way

my breath no longer visible
is a free flock of birds released

above me
the sun
still climbing

and a sky
boundless shelter for my walking
dry as falling leaves.

To see our Truth
is the end of its beginning

to see our false self
is the beginning of its end.

When we are truly flooded with Love
there is no room for bitterness

this is not poetry
but pure biology

our cells are expanding pools
but can only hold so much

Love's eclipse overruns the gutters
breaks the drains with waves of joy
leaves the deck slippery

who walks nearby is likely to fall
become blessed and wet

Love's overflow reaches the lawn
soaks it
life blossoms in the chemistry

this goodness water even reaches
the home where we live
softens the foundation to inspire change

Love-deluge forces choices
decisions about where to come down
from our lofty ecstasy

whether to descend at all

who claims to hold a flood of Love
but carries bitter breezes
may in fact be touched by Love
but only in trickling streams

true flood vacates all else
makes life a living dream
break the levies in your heart
crush the dams and holding pools

you are not a hatchery
you were born to be nuisance
to that which Loves aridity

leave no question as to your
weeping spring
start bawling like a baby

release the geyser long restricted
no one will be left standing
in your wake

they will have slipped
fallen
begun drowning
laughing
in your rising lake.

Great Spirit is blowing
on the embers of your heart
trying to start the fire of your true living

can you feel the rush of Immensity
through the sleeping canyons of your being?

your gray embers flirt over and again
with catching a permanent glow
your essence yearns for conflagration

breath after breath this Great blowing

you are kindling on a damp day
stubbornly you refuse to be lit

this world is cold
we need a fire!

please renounce your smolder
let your temperature rise until
you reach the magical moment
when your field of embers at last
becomes too hot and throws off
its dreary clothes of ash
begins dancing as flames devouring air

finally then Greatness can move on to
lighting epiphany fires
in souls elsewhere.

A flower buds then blooms
a man buddhas then blows away

both have broken free
announcing their fortune
in fragrance that says:

I no longer long
for I am no longer

I have caught the wind
my tender heart dispersed
into those unending waves we greet
at forever's gypsum shores.

Opportunity lies unseen in the dark

only the illumination of our purpose
reveals its cloistered massiveness

we must project our true self
our genuine destiny
onto that shy plant in the corner
of blackened space

our greatness sits
hot and boiling in the vat
of our disbelief in self

it could rampage through night
and lift the curtain on what may be

but first we must pour

we must pour out our greatness
heave our totality
onto the barely breathing fire

its flames will explode
into pillars of brilliance

the shy plant will catch
both heat and light
become fed

when we cast our Divine reason for living
out across space
instantaneously
we bring opportunity
out of the shadows
and trembling sprout
becomes a giant tree
becomes a forest

becomes entirety

our purposeful life
has always been right there before us
our vision has failed to grasp it

purpose is always before us
like a small child
aching for our recognition
not believing that we
cannot see its grandiosity

it—the canyon of ten thousand miles
we—the ant at its edge treading
in fretful circles wishing to encounter
something grand beyond the mundane

no one owns the manuscript
the container
the map
to the hidden treasure
of our singular destiny

it is free of human notion
hovers a faithful Lover
wed to the one who carries its song

only we can own
our providence
the entitlement is ours exclusively

we bray: *if only I could find my purpose*

to Creation this sounds just like

a horse at river's edge
whining for lack of water

purpose need not be found
we never escape its presence

what we need is a flashlight
a torch of courage
a daringness to project
our greatness across space
to shred the dark into
a billion glints of revelation

to thus behold the timid plant
who in the instant of our seeing
transforms into a towering form

a purposeful life must be lived
before it can become purpose
it must be purposed before it can live

this is no chicken and egg story
this law is so old it has lapped itself
in the currents of time

purpose lives in the waiting soil
of self discovery
watered only when we dare to believe
that we were born for a reason
then *leap* toward that reason

can't you hear the music
on the other side of the door?
the party started long ago

you could be inside
and drunk on a fulfilling life

what you bring to the party sits dormant
in a tidy vat composed of your rings of fear

you hold all the liquid light required
to reveal your truth

you were born with the power
to erase darkness and make unseen visible

your vat needs tilting
then one day your freedom

but first you have to pour.

Life Loves us

so it has this to say
by way of reassurance
and explanation:

I am
silent

and that is
why you
scream

if you wish for a more beautiful rain
to fall inside your heart

be what *I* am.

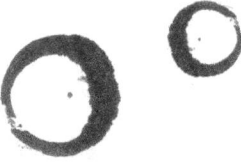

Many moons have passed
but not Love

Love is the lingering mist
destined to stain the sky
and join the soil

the oldest tree
in the most ancient forest
knew the same Love
at its birth
as the Love swirling now
in the youngest orchards

Love has passed through
endless generations of
peach and plum
onto lip and tongue
down the rung

to be yet again
born and sprung
in the awed heart
of old and young

a sturdy drum
is Love

so many hands
have oiled its
equilibrium

go find sorrow
you'll too find Love

and of course in joy's
court and song
Love is hummed

this world is of two notes composed
one the thorn and one the rose

both grow from the stem of Love
both lead blood to run
and hearts to throes

many moons have passed
but not Love.

Knowing that friend is dying to live
friend lights a fire:

I pray that poetry will rush out
of your being in a silver torrent
a river of Divine shouting and whispers
and soak you from the inside out in peace

I drive my knees
bloody and ravaged by the rock
into the gracious dirt
and pray that poetry will drag
its brilliant plow through your tidy
inner palace and decimate the
whole thing to rubble in a flash
of joy's agony and wailing

this is how much I Love you

your soul is a sky of birds
that never stops flying
into the deep expanse of
eternity's elusive mystery

you were never meant to be
grounded like this
pasted against a sullen earth
of capitulation and repetition

and so I pray poetry
will boil in your bones
and bleach your sorrow
into a fine white silt of song
a powder so delicate and tiny
it escapes you easily and always

even when you are in the company
of conventional souls

even when you try with all your might
to fade into the masses of mediocrity

I pray poetry will spray out of you
in a blinding banner of light
and parade you around
a shocked and stooping world
like a carnival freak
forever ending your fantasy of normalcy

I pray poetry will decide
to wait no longer and conducts
an uprising in your soul

it is time for the plantation
on which you have long kept
poetry hostage to your fears
to wither—burn—and die
so that all the slaves that
are your poetry go running
into the river and bless themselves
before crossing over into
the territory of unbridled radiance
that is your light released

I pray that poetry will bother you
mercilessly in this rambunctious way
until you give it your attention
then your permission
and at last your surrender

I pray that poetry
will never leave you alone.

Fresh water perforates my banality
I am leaking laughter and mirth
all over the place

I have been given a thousand new eyes
they bring me such marvelous revelations
like the fact that you friend have always been
a ladybug when before I worried
you were the aphids the spotted lady ate

now I have nothing to fear
you are not so helpless and I am free
to go crazy with my Love affair

my new mistress is named *Surrender*
she has a sister who they call *Letting Go*

you should get to know her.

Under the baobab tree
the gentle sage addresses those
who have gathered restlessly:

You have come to hear me speak
yet quickly grow nervous
then indignant
because you feel I am not
offering concrete solutions

this is like going for a massage
then growing stiff—tense—impatient
because the masseuse is not
reciting a secret recipe
for becoming relaxed

in your misexpectations
you are missing out completely
on the two hands doing healing work
on your battered body

work that would relax you if only
you allowed it to penetrate
and activate your own inherent
mechanisms for relaxation!

I am not the answer
I possess no answer
I do not offer an answer

in my speaking I simply offer
the inspiration that comes through me
praying that it will penetrate you
as do the warmth and energy
of the masseuse's hands
so that something inside of you
comes alive and indicates a way to go

in truth there are no answers
only ways to go
and endless unfolding revelations

but these cannot be offered to you
as an easy platter of *concrete solutions*

we are so self-denying of our own
inherent ability to discover internally
ways toward resolution
we are so trained to seek *answers* from *experts*

expertise cannot be handed over
with a written script
or a list of seven secrets
or top ten traits

understanding is a seed within
waiting for us to soften its husk
with our tears of surrender

waiting for us to feed its flesh with
the massaging light of inspiration

we are not just creative
we are born *creativity*
but such a spark can only be lit
from the inside by our passion-steel
against the flint stone of self belief

do not go to hear someone speak
so that concrete solutions
can be delivered

such things are like perfume
they never smell the same
on one person as another
and what's more
have a way of evaporating
in the air of reality

instead dare to open yourself
and receive the massage of spirit
and its ways of seeing

a force that if it reaches your interior
can erect the most useful signposts
suggesting new ways to go.

L et's say you are suffering

sit down
close your eyes
deep breath

now let all that you believe yourself to be
disintegrate

let it leave you
like sparks from the fire
dancing away into a purifying sky

let your true self burst out in radiant light

this is you
Divine Love

see your light
as it conveys itself
into a large peach on a tree
in an orchard along the belly
of a green valley

now you are the peach
taste of your own sweetness
consume your true beauty

now fat on joy and contentment
fall from the tree onto the soft grass

let your seed be born
into a delightful flower
sweet as a peach
and smiling at the sun.

Life greets us daily with a sublime
and reverberating possibility

should we encounter
in this fragile world
a lesser Love
contorted by suffering and despair

we must be in that eternal moment
the Greater Love

even as our ego flinches for shelter
inside a defensive or hostile husk

we must not wither

either we will be washed over by
that lesser distortion of Love
our bright sand dissolved into
the dark ocean of disharmony

or we will become the forceful tide
our light washing over desolation
drowning it into a sea of ecstasy

as we tread our kindred roads
crossing paths with human souls
this we must suppose

should we encounter in this fragile world
a lesser Love
we must be the silken petal
and not the thorn of rose

in such a moment
when tides on earth are turned
by our heart's conclusion

we must be the Greater Love.

May the ground you walk
rise up to meet your spirit's ascent.

The Divine inscribes Itself
across your face

this is how I say

you are beautiful.

Do you remember the one
about the village that almost died
until it was rescued by a convict?

that's okay
we have time to share the story again . . .

In this village it was dictated that all citizens
must pray with palms touching one another

it was said this would please God
and bring an end to the vicious drought
that had long plagued the people

one day a stir was caused
by the actions of one man
and led the village council to call a forum

the crowd was boisterous in that hot afternoon
their clamor could be heard
from lowly creek to mountain peak

one complainant spoke up:

wise council we have found this man
who has no hands
out in his field praying to God

he has broken the rule of praying
for he has no hands and yet persists
to mock God by praying

how can he receive God if he has not
the tools of proper prayer?

how can he beckon God if he has no hands
for God to notice?

the crowd was uproarious
they could not believe this affront
to their ages-old law for praying

the council hushed the people and called
the accused to testify on his own behalf

with a humble manner and dressed
in modest clothes he rose:

dear wise council
I can only say in my defense
that though I may lack the legally decreed
tools for prayer
that my heart cries out for God

my soul cannot do anything
but lean in God's direction
and spill its every tear in gratitude

I have no hands
but my tools for prayer
do not hang from my limbs
they surge within me

and if you should rule that I am not
allowed to pray with these tools
then I am afraid you will have to kill me

for even if I tried I could not get
my truest tools to stop speaking to God

I could never quiet this endless conversation
with my Divine Companion . . .

people there that day swear that with
these strange and daring words
light broke through the rafters
showering the wise council
in a withering spotlight

wise council ruled amongst themselves
as the people continued to enact

their social drama:

can you believe the nerve?
who could say such a thing?
praying without hands—I have never...
thank goodness the children are in school
he is obviously no true believer

wise council finally spoke:
we have ruled
that though you have clearly violated
our most fundamental ordinance
with regard to faith and prayer
you cannot help your diminished state

and since we are not willing to kill you
in order to prevent your disturbing
manner of prayer
we shall banish you henceforth
to be veiled in silence

no one from this village
shall ever speak a word to you
as long as you live out your days . . .

most people were enraged that this sinner
was allowed to live
but they had high regard for the wise council
and so the clamor slowly crawled back
into the passing of days

the deadly drought continued to cling
to village lands

wise council was forced to go out looking
for a source of food and drink

their village was starving and the end was near

as they forced their emaciated bodies onto the
dirt road leading out of the village
they eventually came upon the property
of the man who prayed with no hands

it was the seventh day from their judgment
a sentencing of banishment into a silent veil

they fully expected to find him now
soiled in shame
his back slumped in sorrow

what they discovered instead
has now become legend

the man was neither soiled nor slumped
but smiling

he stood in the middle of his field
staring at the bright blue rainless sky

his every crop
was propped up on vibrant stalks
and decked out in the most resplendent
leaves of green

his ears of corn were golden and fat
they were dripping juices and laughing

his swarms of melons
looked to burst with sweetness

every legume was plump and growing proudly

dunes of wheat oats rye coriander barley sorghum
piled high and spilled everywhere

almond walnut and cashew trees
drooped from their heavy loads
like weary elders trudging water pails

this man's entire field surged and throbbed
with life

wise council believed it had become delirious
and had passed into a dream

violating their own sentencing—they called out:
banished one—is this field before us real
or have you enlisted dark forces
to play out your anger against us?

banished one smiled yet broader and replied:
I have done no such thing

and yes this field is real
you may come and taste it for yourselves

all I have done is to go on praying
with my true tools of heart and spirit

one morning in the Amazing Grace
of a silence decreed by your collective hand

I woke with a great peace inside of me

when I went out to greet the morning air
this field was growing and beauty I have never
seen before was breaking out everywhere . . .

a long pause ensued between the banished one
who prayed to God with no hands
and the wise council
now wispier than blades of winter grass

at long last
their pride defeated and stomachs roaring
conceit flushed out of their faces as they begged:

do you think you could share your
wealth of food with us dying souls?

banished one replied:
better yet
come and feast and then
I will teach you how to pray . . .

soon crumbs were flying
and juices spraying everywhere

this is how the village
who made a pious man a convict
expelled the narrowness
that kept it from God's harvest

and learned that prayer is a journey
requiring a heart and not two hands.

Some pray kneeling with palms
down against the Earth

some pray with palms
up against the sky

some pray with palms kissing
some with palms at rest on knees

what is all this
but a festival of waving at God?
a billion harvest baskets
carried a billion ways
into which we receive
Divine Bounty

and whether that produce is succulent fruit
from the fingertips of trees
or soil caked vegetables
gestated in womb of earth

we thrill to God waving back

and like child on daddy's shoulders
alongside the parade
our joy rushes over within

for we have waved
and Beauty has noticed.

Have you read the Braille
of an old tree today?

have you stopped?

have you run your calloused palm
and fingers over its thick notes of bark?

could you feel its vibration of a hundred years?

your hand at its trunk—grounded and firm
above—its leaves somber in the wind

could you feel this seduction in your palm
so close to earth?

if not
maybe you should throw off your shoes
and climb
reading the Braille with your bare feet
and palms as you ascend

the bark will speak to you saying:
*nothing moves in you
and where are your rings of growth?
climb higher until you reach my leaves
and lose your groundedness*

climb higher until you reach the dance.

How sweet the taste of sunrise
after the length of bitter night

how glorious the honey wrought
from insect industry

and too the glow of firefly
the consequence of chemistry

collision brings crimson spark from
granite stones

maple runs down only after
tree grows up

old hound dog recalls the pup

sap is sorrowful but feeds
certain souls

deserts dry remember they
were once oceans wet

there is no *is*
there is only *becoming.*

Sometimes
let the tear fall

a note wishes to play itself
inside your heart

let it play.

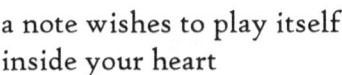

Sky falls as water
dreams grow legs and walk as human

tidal basins grow membranes
across their distal rims
become great earth drums
who express in thunder

garments fray in the heat
their restless threads unravel
take to flight as birds dyed indigo

feathers descend in clouds
clouds leap from water

a child goes dreaming
another emerges from that dream

an ancestor walks among us
disguised as a modern woman
her eyes betray her many moons

many moons live in the womb of sun
many stars flood the plain of space

faces swim in a reunion we do not recognize
our waters have circled through earth and air
to be collected in the stained gourds
we call body
to be poured out over one another
in the precious epiphany of living

so much water looking at itself in wonder
so many yearning pools frightened at
our own reflection peering forth
from our collective aqueous kin

scavenging for the umbilicus
that will lead us back to sea
where freed then lifted
we are sky who cannot help but fall down
as water.

Today I am Loving you

what warmth flashes inside your heart
is affection I weave
into your every moment

a thousand illumined crystals embedded
in your gossamer chamber of soul

I am a mirror who chooses
to bend your way
to shine True Light on you
raising your intrinsic flame
casting you in radiance
to which you so belong

today my heart and soul are singing

you are their song.

There is that which opens the heart
and that which closes the heart
and that is all

no matter the religion—ritual—rhetoric
our earthly light is brightened
or dimmed by a simple choice:

do we choose to Love.

Here is a meditation for you:

envision a field of light
and growing out of it a tree of light
beneath a sky of light

and at the foot of the tree
you
a fountain of light
pouring into a nearby stream of light

pouring into all that is

into all this Light.

Decipher this:

there once was a bird
who discovered it was sky

instantly it lost all concern
for the struggle to fly
for now it knew it was *flight*

dozens of flames lap at the night sky
yet their source is but a singular fire

endless particles of mist
dance out from a glorious waterfall
yet they are protégé of but one single falling

a prairie of cacti owe their birth
to the same sacred soil

seven billion of our kind
are still only the bloom cloud
of just one kind
the Created kind

all multitude is the illusory face of union

know this
practice this
be this
and you will be free

for the ocean is without worry
while each of its droplets
is truly scared to death

come out of your dry isolated mentality
and join the wetness in which you already swim

you will be amazed at what it feels like
to wear the ocean for your skin.

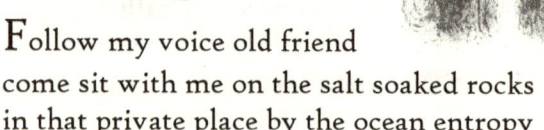

Follow my voice old friend
come sit with me on the salt soaked rocks
in that private place by the ocean entropy

come breathe free with me
on the shorn away rocks that once
were a soft wall above swelling sea

now they rest beside her water
contemplating the vastness of her majesty

soon they will be sleeping and wet
as the stony bed of her marine redundancy

come watch with me
the sun sneak down cloud pocked sky
dropping into its nightly bath in ocean's breast

we will behold the light as it paints
a dazzling streak of diamonds
across the water's dusk-velvet sheet
a glimmering swatch of tides
arcing toward the soft and widowed shore

come smile with me in silence
come let the breeze run across our faces

come be absent from this world with me
and present inside this tidal
proposal between sea and stone

come when you hear my voice
race inside its ancient vibrato

it is a cave leading to this cove
where you may have found
your solace long ago

you can find it there still
still

this place of constant moons
and Love between rocks and water
makes an offering to your tenderness
in seaweed beached and draped on stone

this place is ocean saying:
I have plans for you
I have grown a garden beneath my waves
endless acres of soft and Loving verdancy
dancing in my troupes of water
waiting to massage your deepest untouched
tender spots of soul

walk into my voice old friend
come to that sacred place
where who you are
is touched by sand and sea
and made precious new again.

They greet in the courtyard
beneath the easy palms

two hearts of Love
bowing down to the Divine in each other

they have never met before in this life
though there was a time

now the younger one caresses the palm
of the elder monk and smiling says:

hello flower
you have become a man

monk replies:

yes
and the man grows old

soon I will be a flower again.

A wandering monk encounters a soul
stuck in a morass of mediocrity and rut

monk becomes a beggar
pleading for this suppressed soul
to offer its only real wealth

monk says:
it is not your life that is priceless
my friend
it is your living

breath alone is not enough
be the wind and carry life forward in seeds

live on behalf of life
instead of being just another life
in the way of living

live to increase your liveliness
your vitality and vibrancy

much of living depends on trespassing
through fear's scarecrows to discover what lies
beyond the mind's barbwire boundaries

fear is a premier predator
a life not truly lived is its favored prey

douse your campfire
and wander into the shadows

those shadows are born from light
sun shines beyond your cave

go there and leave your life behind
so that you may achieve the gift of Living.

Another leaf drops gently onto lake
a brown ballerina touching down
all grace and silence

a kiss sent by tree to remind water
of their Love.

When no one is looking
choose Love

in the aching hollows of being
choose Love

before anger's breath
and under the shower of sorrows
choose Love

when judged and scorned
forgotten and abandoned
choose Love

in every hallway of consequence
and breach of peace

for the sake of all that ever
quivers in eternity

surrender every other impulse
unmoor your sacred light
and flying at last into
the alabaster awning of peace

choose Love.

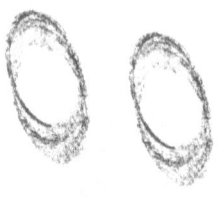

When we encounter one who is suffering
we can say to ourselves:
here is my soul suffering

when we encounter one who is laughing
we can say to ourselves:
here is my soul laughing

in either case
once we have recognized our self in another
our self-Love will respond accordingly

and this world will be new.

That solemn heart pose
of submission and naked Love
that you assume in prayer?

be that
in every moment
before every soul

everywhere.

A note on true friendship:

If you would ask
I would answer

if you would sing
I would echo
I would be the notes
your voice touches
and I would tremble

you need only dream
and my dreams would follow

against your passion tide
my singular sand sweeps away

in your kindly breeze
I cannot but sway

you are a name born long ago
I was at the birthing
and wept at the sound
of your first saying

you are kneeling
I am your praying.

Disrobe your Love

you dear have spent a lifetime
spinning a chrysalis around
your inner form which is formless
tossing shadows onto your
true light which is shadowless

you have chosen a timid valley
for your permanent residence
even though you inherited
citizenship to a mountaintop

for all your thirst
you keep chewing dust

for all your hunger
you bypass the feast of moments
and chase your tail through
the mist of fears

when was your last good meal?

that quicksand you call your property
is doing what quicksand does

who shall retrieve your bones?

build a proper shelter on solid ground
so you can dismiss the vultures
circling over you

cease your ceaseless itinerary of tasks
that keeps you from having to face
the Truth moment that is taskless

disassemble your walls
open your windows
let through the thoughtless sky

acquaint yourself with nothingness
and the sweet orchard of acquiescence

bask in your own true sun
that can never burn you
stop depending on the outside weather

a brook of peace runs through your land
go sit beside its flow and let it be your music

you always were your own greatest
composer and lyricist
yet you persist in purchasing
foreign music and suffering the
twinge of derailed notes

you have a friend who can pull up
all your inner weeds

this friend goes by the moniker:
Sweet Release
and shuns all your favorite clothes.

Willowy I say your name
inside my heart
and your name unfolds its crystal delta
across the place in me that waits for rain

that ground long ago interrupted
in threads of thirst grasping at subtle sky

secretly
I say your name and it becomes a prayer
for something too large to remain a
secret any longer

wistfully I kick my legs in your marsh water
stirring your bath in amber setting sun

in time a crooked piece of driftwood passes
having broken free of something
somewhere upstream

later it will lodge in soil
or submerge in the shallows
either way becoming joined again
like the reeds rustling just a little
on the cool marsh banks

willowy
I whistle your name across
the small diameter of my hollows
where your name
which is the wind
becomes a graceful note
in the song soaking this dry terrain.

You friend are a finder of things
over which to become anxious

choose a new occupation

what you are a finder of
you will find

what you are a loser of
you will lose

I knew a man who was a loser of worries
and a finder of joy

his eternal smile
gave the sun its name.

You
beloved
are anxious

to learn what it means to be without anxiety
spend time with that which is not anxious

so many anxious people suffering their anxiety
desperate to be relieved yet choosing
to be around other anxious people
other anxious technologies

nervous cups pouring into nervous cups
bewildered as nervousness increases

meanwhile nature is perplexed

it offers us a world of peaceful companions
each waiting for us to take a calm walk together
and see what serenity can truly be.

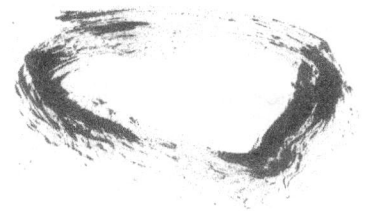

Sky is another form of ocean
ocean once lived as a tree

these elements recognize their kinship
in the seeing that is without thought

sensate connectedness is their birthright
as it is ours though we are flooded with
thought and cannot see

our dense flesh once danced ethereal
in the nebula and streamed through space
yet we believe we are composed
separately from and foreign to
this natural world

we are the natural world's clay crafted
into form of flesh

we are a sacred rearrangement of
all the old gardens and crumbled mountains

we too are a variation of the ocean
our particles once stood tall in
the form of cypress trees
fell seasonally as leaves

the veins in our hands are offspring
and ancestor to veins in every leaf

we are a temporary posing of clouds
turning forever into our next expression
in the turbulence and alchemy of Creation

we came from everything
and give birth to everything

we occupy a peculiar moment in the cycle
staring out at all that we once were
and are destined for again
beholding it all as a foreignness when
it could not be more intimately in us
of us

oh how we could discover our true family
and revel in the union
if only we would learn to see
with a nakedness of thought

like the way a moonflower gazes
at the moon
believing entirely that it is gazing
into the clearest mirror
there ever could be.

Remember when we were walking
in passion's garden
and lavender was throwing a party?
remember coriander dancing clumsy
and mint drunk on pepper seed?

remember when you exploded delightfully
became a screen of pollen aloft in breeze
that sun shone through?

or hibiscus giving up its head
to the guillotine of silence
all so sameness could be circumcised
and sepia could blush into royal color?

in the bird bath
that's where our dreams collided
and winged promises came crawling forth
wet and surrendered to the ceaseless narrative
whose only utterance is *BE*

do you remember our walk in passion's garden?
remembering would rain down on your slumber
and release your drumbeat dormancy

remember . . . friend . . .
catapult up through reams of sleep
and burst out through the final awakening
into who you were born to *BE*.

Are you ready for the ocean of oceans?

you say you want true joy
to flood your soul plain

first you will need to let all of *this*
become nothing
so that everything
can be born again

the birth wail will be enormous silence
the placental glisten a sky of mirrors
a galaxy of crystals sparkling out
from infinity's sand

are you ready for the source of suns?

once you kiss this Light
you will be annihilated
and nightingales will hear of you
the one who drank the potion brewed by eternity
to court all lambs who bleat toward Love

you
the one who blasphemed
against human sensibility
walked naked into moonlit tide
and . . . with conformity's clothing left behind
drank the vintage wine

losing inhibition and virginity
to the tender thrust of Peace.

Forest is a cane flute God's lips play
to resounding tribute

sacred breath runs along the trees
brushing its wind against bark
sparking up such music
so ecstatic the outcry

everywhere on earth this delirious symphony
this breeze threading stems and blades
over and again through seasons
never the same note reborn

all the opuses of mortals cannot touch
this ultimate siren

though the rebels and runaways rush to it
following the river
enchanted through the long night
by soliloquy from within

and bright moon dips its eyes
turns its ears
never without wonder at the impossible music
of the cane flute swept through by Love

and the silence after.

Why take a matter of your soul
before the court of one whose soul is suffering?

why bring your broken heartedness
to a heart breaker?

if we seek a thing
we should go to the source of what we seek

instead we so often kneel downstream
from sewage pipes in fetid waters and drink
when our every cell is dying for the purity
of a mountain spring

mountain goats know to climb
when predators approach
they flee to pinnacles
where they cannot be reached

why do we so often leap
right into the lion's mouth?

we say we're heading north
so why are we walking south?

we say we want peace
yet we practice turbulence

what spirit-student has ever made this work?

what the mind focuses on it unleashes
how about some light?

dogs bark because they are not cats
cats do not play catch
they are not dogs

why do we expect a scattered life
to bring us centeredness?

loneliness is not the absence of company
it is the presence of *dis-ease*
with the only company
we can ever truly keep

so why do we run from the one relationship
that can never leave us?

we are the bizarre face of paradox
even as we apply our mascara of logic

birds high in trees wonder about us
even as we are so certain of our superior state

we state our cause for hate
to the ones we Love
blind to the beginning of their soul-death
instigated by the world tour of our enmity

we want the world to be more Loving
so why do we release balloons of bitterness
that burst at altitude and rain acid recklessly?

a child sees a flower
and falls in Love with that wondrous being

we see a flower and fall into fretfulness
over the task from which we believe
the flower distracts us

we return calls from others
but not from our soul
that rarely catches us at home

we catch butterflies but not compassion
though butterflies only want to be free of us
and compassion only wants to make
our heart its home

to come inside our home
a visitor first must have our trust

yet we will let anyone come inside our peace
and tear up all the furniture

we glance at each other
waiting to see who will smile first
but could not care less whether our scowl
is preceded by another's

we laugh so hard our tension vanishes
then react as though our laughter is inappropriate
and tension is proper adult attire

a tire stops working when it needs fixing
why won't we?

a tree heals itself because it can
why don't we?

a cloud cries when its heart is heavy
why do we hoard our rain?

we have a notion of who we are
we will not let that notion *be*

we send our anger out into the world
with no limits or curfew
but we keep our kindness locked up inside

we use the word *friendship* loosely
the word *hate* freely
the word *Love* tightly
honor hardly
oneness barely

gossip pours out of us
true praise stays in us

we'll spend all day looking out the window
yet won't step outside the window
and look back in

sun sets
night falls
sun rises
night recedes
this is good couples counseling

snow falls—lands—then rises
this circle could be our teacher

rain falls—flows—follows a path back to sky
master teacher!

preacher bellows
pew creaks
peace settles in the grooves of our silence

why are we so loud?

what we fear is a flame surrounding
what we need

maybe it is time to burn

days are a teacher

a child might say:
it's time to learn.

Open your eyes friend
gently peel back the petals
of your mind's rose flower
and let your tender idea of this world
take on light

watch as the ladybugs of peace and serenity
descend to your soul-stalk and begin consuming
your blight of fear and lifelong farming
of self-defeating inner language

those persistent aphids stand no chance
before the appetite of actual seeing

as you learn to keep sight of the endless
shifting roots of your dismay
and the infinite reasons for joy
laced into the translucent web of being
your very tracking
your awareness
will be like fresh water spread
on pregnant ground

new beauty will sprout from your thoughts
bright blossoms will fall from your mouth
and your actions will fulfill your desire

for such is our fortune when we scuttle
old and useless blinders
fastened when we were young

such is our life's revolution
when we part the rose bud
and court the Light of rampaging union
that would Love nothing more
than to romance our melancholy
into a skyward elation.

Those who assail us bless us
for they offer us the anvil against which
we pound ourselves into our truest form
the form that allows our flight into purpose

those who do us harm offer us the fire
that can soften our metal for the pounding

a sculptor's gleaming chisel and rasp
and the farmer's trusted plow blade
were first poor unproven pieces of scrap
wanting—yearning for a magmatic bath
in the forge's inferno

then for the cold hardness of anvil
and crush of merciless vice

finally for the kiss of hammer
and the intimate friction of polishing

what shines even in daylight
first has been attacked blessedly
in the dark smog and soot
of the blacksmith's shed

what rises up out of injury
could not have risen unless it first
recognized the opportunity presented
by the cruel serving of pain

unless first translating that cruelty
into the pleasure of transformation

let us take hurtful words and actions
the projectiles of another's foul dreaming
and use them to smelt our steely self
into a graceful flowing corona
whose light teaches the careless weavers
that they too have spun our heaven.

Dissolve into light and Love
become absent from flight of arrows

become the garden where malice
cannot enter

choose the essence of that rare
and priceless flower
that emanates a higher luster
offering pestilence and its sword of spite
not a single petal on which to land

life is so much sweeter
lived not as form
but as fragrance
that essential oil escaped to air.

When a thing catches fire
we can do one of two things:

we can put the fire out
preserving what is burning
and what the fire will eventually consume

or we can allow the fire to do what fire does:
destroy what has been
to give birth to what will be

fire is life's great *untamer*

a lion tamer trains the powerful beast
against its true nature

what once lived a brilliant feline acuity
of sensation—perception—action
is dulled into a melancholy

of stimulus and response
at the behest of a foreign whip and voice

what once was internally alive
has become externally dependent

the charismatic has become habitual dimness
phenomenon is reduced to puppet

this is what lion tamer does to greatness

a thousand lion tamers
prowl the jungle of human lives
and human societies

they seek the lion within us

the crowd they play to is our fear and ego
who cheer fanatically at the tamer's
conquering of our own soul

faithfully we sell out this stadium of docility
drawn by a sales pitch promising
a safe and wealthy life

we each are born with souls of lions
when it comes to stalking our potential
and gashing open false skins of idea
to get at the flesh of true life

then come days and suspect conversations
then comes insidious forgetting
and through this pallid murmuring
of lies and disappearances

the stalker we were born to be
becomes the stalked we are

lion becomes listless and languor

lion tamers tell us to tamp out
brushfires of the soul
lest they grow into wildfires
and set the soul free

instead they encourage the kind of fires
that kill our dreams
molesting us to strike the match of fear
and inflame the collective fields of aspiration
so dry under our drought skies of doubtfulness

we so often oblige
running from soul fire
imagining the comforts it will burn
and not the awakening that will be born

grieving what might be removed
underestimating what soul fire invites

absent of this burning
our emotional and spiritual underbrush
accumulates in tall piles and thick tangles

we are caught in place in knots and snares
sensing what it means to be free
howling wailing whimpering
but not choosing to do the one thing
to destroy the underbrush that claims us

life cannot help its compassion
and so it offers us fire:
the great untamer
the force that kills complacency
and with fresh air fertilizes ground
to summon the sprouting of new seed

there is that which should be preserved
and that which by fear and habit
we desire to keep alive

when a thing catches fire
we can do one of two things

when your own soul catches fire
dear one . . .

let it burn!

A lifelong musician shatters her instrument
in a moment of understanding

tears fall in soft staccato notes
and deep yearning at long last cries out:

I seek the music of emptiness
the mattress for my spirit rest

I must truly lose my head
to join the passion wild things know

the galloping surrender into stillness
the silent waterfall of soul in flow

our modern heads are mad chambers
where all drunken musicians and malcontents
gather to screech their disharmony

foolishly we invite them free of charge
to set up camp in our garden
to ply their screeching

they pull up our flowers and spawn our weeds
their noise chases away quiet butterflies
attracts rancorous roaches and fleas

Buddha must shake his head at us
conducting such chaotic symphonies

but would we let these clatter souls
leave our soil and let their tools to rust
we might encounter true music
silence strung in heavenly chords

we might catch the conversation between
rock—snail—and underbrush

this is why true teachers cleave themselves
of their heads and lay askew
laughing in shade of almond trees.

Transient trawls a lantern across
June's newborn summer night sky

its glow crawls behind clamoring
of treetops fussing at hot gusts
barely cooled since day

transient pulls the beaming orb
through forests of shadows
baiting our attention
to the burgeoning mystery
of a persistent womb
cycling once more toward birth

playful moon ushering out a sweet calypso
soothing serious creatures
such as us to remember
the lightness of darkness
when tasks pause before eclipsing waves
and what we thought was urgent is revealed
as another flash through constellations

wispy brief firebird here spectacular
then gone . . . then simply gone

caustic moon
washing away atmospheric blemishes
scrubbing extinct the idea that nothing lives
while we sleep toward
dawn's revival of worries

aproning moon in cute curtsy before clouds
wiping its hem of accumulated month
dashing flour as a pollen burst
out into black suspended plains
dashing not flour but stars

new arrivals of imminent departure
flashing exhibitionists bolted against
a dark wall that stands
only when sun is seated

arid moon urging us to cry wonder
and splash our tears upward
to penetrate its loneliness
even amongst a sky of peers

noble moon enduring our ignorance
our chaotic dismissal of its cycling narrative
its silent sonnet desiring
that we stop and look

a transient trawls this lantern
some sort of reunion
29 days in waiting
languorous roll of egg through womb
cloaked pangs
muted moaning

vernal divulgence
crescendoing hour of prebirth
milk of light diffusing
suckling of the nocturnals

suckling that is
when we choose to wake
in the illuminated black
of worlds who are not sleeping.

Fear
is not knowing how close
to dying you are
yet carrying a spirit who
whispers to you that
one thing is true:

you are far from living

living
is knowing how much you
risk by Loving
and Loving anyways

wanting to stand on familiar ground
at the edge of comfort's canyon
but falling nonetheless

having every reason to grow hard and cold
become a petrified forest of stoniness
yet choosing to live in tenderness.

A morning mantra for remembering:

I am a descendent of myself
emerged from each moment of my living

I am my own ancestor
the progeny of my giving

I am the offspring of my becoming
and of my failure to become

I am what I have poured out
and the absence of my pouring

I am the echo of my every thought
the condensation of thoughts manifest

I am a waterfall
life is the shelves I splash over

I am the vapors from my dreams
and the dreaming of my vapors

I am laughter remembered
and tears resurrected

I am the gamble
and the gasp at the hand

the sorrow bundled in texture
the space between sand

I am clover at sunrise
myrtle at the noon

the tremble at consummation
the breath after breathing too soon

I am the blade at the head of the dozer
the plow at the burrow's back

I am both
I am neither

I am ether
I am glider

I am sniff
and then scent

blow
and then dent

I am the weed that keeps blooming
the yarn for the looming

the story leaked out
across ages of pages

the flood of the valley
the life that comes after

the sugar
the salt

the dust in the rafter

breeze rinsing air
passion brimming in lair

I am the secret
the sharing

the fear
and the daring

I am the Love
making Love
making
Lovemaking.

If you find yourself frustrated
at the constant darting about
of the lizard

do not blame the lizard

it is being what it is

for stillness
my beloved
go and find a tree!

Sky speaks:

I am blue sky
unfolding without notion
airborne ocean

I cannot be touched
though I touch all things

I cannot be harmed
though harm passes through me

I am not joy
though joy blooms in me

I am the silent murmur
that never ends

I remain after the showers
stand still in the storm

I am formless
though I host all forms

I am not the dream
though I make dreaming possible

I have no boundary
no dimension
carry no apprehension

wind seems to stir me
this is no illusion

forms seem to obscure me
this is your delusion

I cannot be made less or more
cannot be diluted—uprooted—distorted

I am endless birth
not ever aborted

I am always shining
for I forever host the sun

at times you do not recognize my light
you are blinded by cloud and night

I am not what you name me
but I am what I am:
lamp—lantern—light—flame

I am regardless

perceptions change
I remain

I am blue sky
all these clouds are yours
dismiss them
discover you are blue sky too.

So many open windows...
and Love's divine breeze aloft to carry us

endless blooms of airy moments
each saying: *Come this way
I will birth you unto yourself*

Soul's response: *I will.
For I am blue sky
and I am returning home.*

There are some things inside us
that speak out and say:

release me as a poem.

The conversation should always start with

Peace.

We are so desperate to believe
in our separation from the world
that we do not recognize our own family
gathered around us in form of the natural world

our ancestors the mountains and boulders
tuckered out and banked in their chairs
staring out over the porch of valleys
watching as we run around the yard
frantic children thinking we are grown

but a mountain stone knows what it means
to be truly grown

our relatives the natural world
they throw fits and squabble just as us
how else the squawk of quail in underbrush?

and for all our emotions we are not so unique

for instance:

roses blush

I have seen
no
caught scent of their color flush
all shy and awkward when spied by us
embarrassed as we make such a fuss
lifting petals up to our dreamy inhale
purring at the sweet perfume released
when the bashful petals sense our crush

roses blush.

Do not endeavor only to be a national treasure
nations burn and age and lose their lines

nations dissolve away and into each other
no more sturdy than sand amid sand
at the mercy of a wind revival

do not be so small and shifting

be more than a national treasure
be a global jewel

your shine and heft will appreciate over time
as the world turns over on itself naturally
burnishing your offering into a yet finer prize

being a Lover of nation has its initial worth
and can feel good enough during a lifetime

but that breed of Love is a water
that does not leave its well

this earth wants to be watered
through its entire being

it is a garden crying to the human spout:
now come over here to my neglected leaves!

break open your well of nation-Love
and water the world that is your fuller self
your forgotten land
your receded peoples continuing your story
absent of your audience

you should join the show
you might discover that your many faces
are beautiful
that they dream and weep as you do

why drink your milk from such
a narrow glass of identity?

why pucker your mind-lips closed so far?

the milk cannot get in
it curdles on the cold floor
staying where you spilled it

open your mind's mouth all the way
and drink!

nation-Love is often popular
easy thinking calls it patriotism
without examining Love's true intent:
to be diffused
to be surrendered
not to be encased in coffins of territory
and possession

nation-Love is a swell in the ocean
it is not the ocean—that endlessness
rich with worlds

nation-Love is an approximation of true Love
it is a step
it is not the staircase

nation-Love has potential when it is freed
to become world-Love
to be joined back with itself

patriotism is not Love of nations
it is Love of world reflected in nation
such that nation becomes a nest from which
we take flight into our human contribution

do not flirt with the moon
then strafe the stars with bullets of disregard

moon is lit by a star
moon has relationship with stars
moon and stars go way back

moon would never deny its people—the stars
so how can we deny our own people:
humankind and world kind?

we fall in Love with what is near
blind to its birth from what is far

ignorant to the kinship whose fieldwork
graces our daily table with bounty of every kind

let the magistrates quibble over boundaries
of nation devotion

you are the court's bailiff
guard life's proceedings
unholster your armament of identity
pick up the staff of light
wave it over every living thing

this case comes down to Love

Love does not run up to boundary and cease
Love explodes boundary and shreds
every single territorial lease.

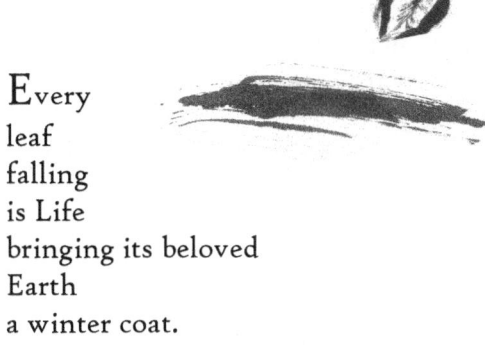

Every
leaf
falling
is Life
bringing its beloved
Earth
a winter coat.

From the shelves of desert thrones
plateaus whispering whistling
as Great Spirit blows by
settles a warmth on this day
around the forms of
Grandmother and Grandson

and Grandson
perched on a sturdy lap
asks:

Grandma
how old are you?

Grandmother raises an eyebrow
gathers galaxies in her eyes
turns her glance toward child:

how old am I?
I am younger than the moon that
danced last night for you

I am younger than the stars
that let Spirit light shine through

younger also than their sister Sun
who bakes us warm on this blessed day

you drank from that stream over there
and climbed that willow tree
and that canyon rock

I am younger than all of those
younger too than the rain
the seasons
this desert
these mountains that frame our view

I am younger even than the genes
that reside inside of you

you see—my child
you could as easily ask how young I am
for in many ways I am infancy

Grandson was confused by this

but Grandma if you are young as all of this
then what am I?

I am now three years old
and I thought I was a big boy

Grandmother again paused
to gather galaxies in her eyes
then reassured this way:

you *are* a big boy my child
you are ancient as the sand
that settled around newborn pyramids

you were present when life
first crawled from sea

you knew the chill of space
before light first shone

you were rusted weary
when Kublai Khan took the throne

your long and flexible arms
plucked fruit from prehistoric trees

you sat in primordial grass
and witnessed the continents first divide

you helped blow motion
into a still universe
this gave spin to moon
entranced the ocean tide

you see—my child
we are both at once aged and youthful
wise and greatly naïve

for we have traveled far in both directions
along the circle of Spirit Road

this is why though my skin is wrinkled
my laughter comes like a fresh spring
spouting from the enchanted babe

and this is why Truth has convened
over and again in your eyes
and you often utter tenured speech
even though your baby skin
as yet unmarked
shames in its smoothness
even this perfect peach

Grandma spoke these things

and this is how
on this day
on a desert plateau
a three year old
came to know his boundlessness
and the intimacy of a dance we call Time.

Wading into waters unknown
begins with a shifting in the heart
long before movement finds our legs

inertia is a beauty we serenade
until it swells and fills our cup
scales down its castle wall
to settle within us

the peasant dreaming
of what life is beyond the moment
whose ground we have trodden

the garden whose soil we have leached
the time whose circles we have worn bare

move
we say
to our own stillness
it does

move

we are brave now
leaves turn
even as buds stir within the branch
eager for the spring

we will meet that warm season
at its birth
for now we are motion
as all things living should be

smile creases the face of our desire

even as we splash the puddles of change
into clouds of anxiety
we are coming clean

even as we strain to
un-become this weary note
we are learning a new song

a song first sung
by a shifting in the heart.

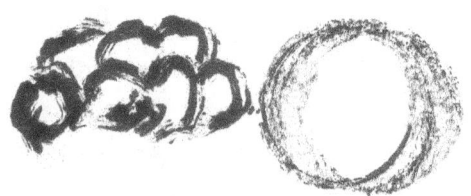

One seeker to another:

Please friend do not slam your hard mind
into my tender message

let go

allow my words to drift gently and fall
cherry blossoms onto the dewy grass
of your heart

your mind can be a fist
tight and sure of itself
yet ill-formed for anything but punching

your heart's lawn is full of promise
it was shaped for catching tears
and turning them into flowers

please let me weep into you
these seeds of marigold

your own Loving nature will fertilize
their journey thereafter

do not go scurrying for the nearest shade
to hide inside

we are not mice or roaches
our family of beings seeks the sun

be like doves and turtles
find a warm flat rock
on the water of this message

dry off from blindness
bask in the sun
let its intensity which is Love
penetrate your defenses

melt your resistance into a puddle
of what you used to be

I have no impressive knowledge
this is not your encounter with genius

I am but a shy cloud
who has an arrangement with sky
to let sun come through.

Love *is* life
hatred is the disruption of life

Love is the nature-state of living things
hatred is the poisoning of that nature-state

Love is the flow of spirit energy
between and between
hatred is the halting of the spring

they are not two sides of the same coin
nor are they both innate to living

one is given before even the first breaths
of life in the time when spirit flows
with spirits among worlds

the other descends from the translation
of foul energy through gaping wounds
into a reason for bad intentions

hatred is taught
most assuredly so

Love is the inescapable impulse as central
to life as is silk to the web

Love *is* life
hatred is the disruption of life

the solution is apparent friend:
let's get a life!

Y ou are a camel

please do not be offended
I just mean that you use your Love-water well

you carry it preciously
share it graciously
and somehow travel long distances
without running dry

most of us spill our drink carelessly
and grow thirsty every seven steps.

Symbiosis:

the divine kiss of life
making Love to itself
in endless disguise.

A new moment is born
right now!

be blessed in it

do not wait for rain to disappear
into earth before you open
your mouth to sky to taste it

take it in while it is falling!

now another moment arrives
jump into it

the time for Joy is wherever a moment
shows itself

moments are not like wild animals
we do not have to go looking for them

they are not prairie dogs
popping up from their dens
disappearing at our approach

moments are in us
emerge from us
dance all around us
waiting to be seen

waiting for us to join the celebration.

A poet composed his masterpiece
and waited proudly in the courtyard
to recite it to the masses

not a single person arrived

discouraged
the poet decided to recite his
great work anyway

at that very moment God flew by
as a sparrow
heard the beautiful recitation
and smiled

the poet trudged home
saddened and deflated
his dreams of adulation evaporated
in the knifing absence of attention
he had imagined for himself . . .

our true tragedy is when we confuse
the audience of masses with that
within us that pleases God.

[alternate ending]:

only one simple soul arrived
in the courtyard
a street sweeper dressed in
tattered burlap clothes

the street sweeper was enamored
by the poet's masterful expression

he went home and recited the poem
to his beloved wife with whom he was
suffering a long drought of affection

at the beauty of the poetry
the man and wife fell in Love
with each other as they had when
their skin was young and smooth

now their heart wrinkles obliterated
into tenderness
kindness flowed between them
an obstructed river at last released . . .

do not count your audience
simply go about the world
spilling your beauty everywhere

a starved soul may come 'round
and lap it up with the greatest of gratitude.

Become as the honeybee
who goes after nectar
and picks up pollen along the way

go after the sweet essence of nothingness

this way you will acquire peace
without even trying

better yet
your hive will buzz in sheer delight
at your return

for you will have brought back
a lightness of union
now rippling through their hearts

a mysterious wave cleaving
them from their heavier mood

enticing them to dance
like the bees they were born to be.

Come
warm your hands
on the fire of your soul

it burns for you
will you let its torrid infatuation
have some measure of satisfaction?

it would make a good Lover
confirming your truer beauty
in countless strokes

it would say to you
I understand
each time your torn heart
cried for validation

your soul is there for you
an eternal friend
steadfast Lover
speaker of all you long to hear

but your ear
your ear is tuned to the world
and all its many frantic waving hands
each saying: *come this way*
we'll show you a real blaze

you fall in Love with a sweeping fable
and you go its way

when you arrive you discover
no fire ever existed there

nothing resides in that place but cold
and damp and boundless hollows

your fingers freeze and ache
next to chill is your heart

all your false friends have now fled
you are lost and alone in woods of despair

shivering and starving
frightened and panicked
you seek shelter for the long night ahead

but then Grace
a wondrous glow peeks forth
through the elders

you stagger that way
curious
clinging to your last resolve

closer now
you encounter the truest friend
you will ever know

at last you sit and warm your hands
on the fire of your soul . . .

this tale is so familiar
because it is the human story

we have been spinning it repeatedly
like a forgetful grandfather
pleased with himself
for his originality.

Sometimes it is enough simply to gaze
upon the face of beauty for a moment
and say inside the heart

I am blessed.

Peddler meets sojourner
at a characteristic bend in the road

the predictable question comes:

what can I sell you?

and the response:

I seek the sap of Creation
the nameless *Allness* that dews the vine

please rid me of this universe
of persuasions and appearances

let my soul break through the crust
and be blistered in the pie-filling of essence

my head hurts from the buzz of conformity
the countless *supposed to's* that fly off
from interminable scores of tongues

I want the mountain when it was bare
and not littered with our signposts and flags

such a forlorn road we tread
our satchels so emptied and yawning

our sustenance so heaped high and waiting
strewn across our unfolding acres

and yet our minds possessed by
the easy jewelry
fast application
symbols parading our club's self-approval

oh these many clothes
that steal our nakedness

a river of tea stewed of bark and bristle
runs nearby our camp

we go walking
atremble as we leave the comfort of fire

we hear a glorious water running
but are torn at this point of no return

we dream of drowning in the tar pitch
of a genuine current depth
and yet the campfire we have always known
beckons to us

we believe we are cold when in fact
we are only dying into the cusp of birth

coldness becomes an idea
that we conclude of ourselves

this is the moment of our frightened decision
to *not* make it to the edge of water
and behold our revelation

we have chosen the pantomime warmth
of the false flames we have known

the retreat back to camp is quick
our arrival greeted by the applause
of many who also hear the near rapids
but maintain a costly affair with suffering

ideas of God are the kindling we are given
for our minds are addled with an addiction
to rules and conventions

but no kindling ever fallen has become
True Flame
without the breath of Essence

or to speak another way
we mistake wood for fire
and water for drowning

you have to light a thing to make it burn
we must open up and swallow
to be filled with the blessing of the sea

we dear sojourners make festivals
out of bark and branch
grow drunk on leaves
pass out beneath tawdry canopies
rise at morn hung over
from impure consumption

these parties are fun at certain points
but I seek the sap of Creation

the exploding taste that lives
beneath all commotion
and leaves me dripping
after the celebration of rules is done
and the party goers are parched
and dry as stone

good peddler
you cannot sell me what I seek
for glory water has no proprietor
and its only price is my movement
toward the always running creek.

Wisdom without compassion
results in arrogance
and self-consumption

compassion without wisdom
is like tossing medicine
into the wind.

Human Being
A Definition:

a physical manifestation or expression
of the energy of the universe
such that a tangible system of body
and mind may serve as vessel
for emotions—thoughts—spirit

all of which have as purpose
the movement of larger humanity
toward awareness of itself through both
individual growth and generational evolution

to be human is therefore our exercise of Spirit

a voyage of person growth
into the enormity that is soul

so that while we may be partial product of
and partially bound by an imperfect system
of fears—emotions—thinking
we may allow the Spirit of Life
and the Divine Purpose of Creator Force
to assume precedence and prominence
in this physical dimension

this human being
a spirit cloud cloaked in human form
is cloud of cloud
spirit of spirit
strand in the web of life

an inseparable particle of universal oneness
not superior to or apart from other life
but brother to the waters—lands—skies
sister to the animals—plants—peoples
kin to the planetary bodies

composed of the same matter
as all that has been and will ever be

a distinct condensation of energy
gifted with a particular consciousness

indelibly interflowing with the impulses
of pain and joy
positivity and negativity
creation and destruction
that permeate the quilt of this totality

as one human exhales
so inhale all others

as each extends
all others receive

to be human is to be a work in progress
to seek reflection of one's own image
in the relatedness and distinctiveness
of all of Life

a human in being is a cocoon
harboring the growth of a place within
where the spirit may enter in full form
with wings ready for flight toward
self-recognition and partaking of
the larger revolution of Life
toward its own awareness

it is a gestation of fear—uncertainty—pain
discovery—passion—and grasping imperfection
inside the mighty currents of *becoming*
toward reunion with Divinity

a human being is a spirit
first and last

by this definition
wherever one person may come across
or consider another
peace and respect must above all else
be in order

for a human is being

a human is being.

Fill your mind with flowers
do not imagine them there
realize them—create their vivid flesh
infusing the lawn of your mentality

this is not make believe
it is *believe to make*

the silver fish contains the lake
leaves contain the rake
your mind already contains what it needs
to soothe you from your clinging ache

transformation is borne of brine
concludes sublime in this curing vessel

are you sad my friend?
fill your mind with flowers

there is a reason for their sweet bouquet
inhale—they will carry you through your day

if your day stretches dreary before you
fill your mind with flowers
flags of a dreamy God
they were born colorful for a purpose
look deeply—let them dazzle you
with their kaleidoscope display

your mind is not a vacancy idling
it is a sponge and waiting

not a helpless teacup
into which you pour your daily worries

rather a muscle made for lifting mundane
weight into mystical joy

your mind
a sunspot flaring endlessly

in a billion years you will see that
in this very moment it was waving at you
saying:

beloved soul—fill me with flowers
I will be your garden
together we will live in paradise
smiling at butterflies
who come to stay awhile
where Beauty grows.

May you find those precious flowers
hidden in the vastness of every moment

bow down to sit with them
learn their lovely faces
enjoy their fragrant story

allow them to douse you
warmly and quietly
with their uncelebrated
beauty of being.

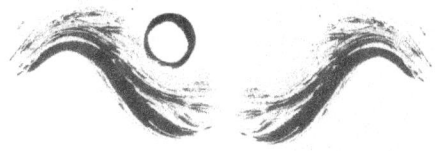

Shepherd reasons with a poor listener
on a hillside:

please cousin do not confuse my words
they are very clear as to
what they mean to say

my words are heading through a valley
toward a mystical mountain
with plains wide and free as the palms of Life

you are doing your best to herd them
through tight narrows in tall canyons

you have your own plans for them
once you have them in your corral
your miniscule space of reasoning
camouflaged by a sharp thicket
of prejudicial chaparral

you have plans for my words
that you did not actually originate

for those notions were born in the generations
that have passed on your fear to you

you are so intent on driving my words
harder than they are meant to be driven

across distances they are not meant to cover
without proper water—food—rest
when all they want is stillness
so you can be with them in silence

maybe spend a night under a bright black sky
encamped around a warming fire

you are doing your best with this moment
but the generation echo
that dominates your mind
leaves you deaf to the carpet of song
I weave for you

leaves you
unable to receive the Loving thread
leaves you left from the loom

so now here we are you and I
beneath the brawn of glaciers
each needing something small and delicate
such as a word
to lean upon

we both could use a bath
to cleanse ourselves

I have heard of one

it is a hot springs located
along the fault lines
of true communication
that just so happen to run through
a wide-open plain

if you can muster the emptiness
needed for true listening
I can take us there

please do not confuse my words
they are very clear
as to what they mean to say.

In this country we need to practice smiling

too often shrouds canvas our faces
depression sinking us deeper tick by tick

smiling costs us nothing other than risking
perceived foolishness
birds laughing at us
or some such mess

but what is ridicule when stacked against
mountains of misery?

we should practice smiling in every moment
even when protocol says frown

so deep is our frowning habit
with each long face worn then worn again
we teach our bodies—hearts—and souls
to adopt this countenance

muscles remember their most frequent salute
begin to soldier their fibers such

the marching orders pass on to nerves
where spirit picks them up

we might as well be puppets wooden
our will to lightness leaves us so
we grow stilted
bereft of mirth

living things look at us and wonder
why the endless dour face?

they ask amongst themselves:
don't humans know that even pain
is full of Grace?

all of nature roots for us to loosen up
break the facial ice and smile

for a smile lets the breeze of joy
enter the soul
where warmth gets made

song then fertilizes in the deepest chamber
music finds the mouth

smile lets the breeze of joy come in
smile lets the music out

smile infects bland souls walking
festival takes the day

even when we drink our tea
smile
look closely

tea will smile back

all the world is waiting
to be warmed.

Even a blade of grass
has something to teach
one who is looking to learn

even the invisible
has something to show
one who is looking to see

we do not live a beautiful life
because we happen to find beauty
but because we choose to *be* beautiful

you
friend
are a living field of flowers
wishing someone would
buy you a rose!

Something without boundary
and possessed of life-giving breath
speaks into the marrow of a beautiful one
languishing in the margins
of what her life *could be:*

Your soul pours out now
you've suffered so long and all you needed
was to stop your madness of motion
and sit beside the grass

see how I have made it a shocking green
for you?

see how I have tinted the light
as if in a dream?

this waking life is the true dream
a fantasy if you let it be as such

let go the chaos of lost souls
don't join that parade

I created you for the ecstasy of dissolving
in long baths of solitude
so that your soul may awaken
to its belonging with all things

you must walk through the blistering
waterfall of loneliness
absolute chilling aloneness
before you reach the other side
where I make days a dream

the souls who circle you chattering
these are your angels at the work
of deciding how to entice you to hear
true music and leave alone the noise
of human wailing

bear for a moment the pain of separation

once you tear your self from flesh
you will open up into your final fantasy
realizing only then that you have always
been in the company of Creation
you could not be less alone

you are at the center of the largest party
here there is no *other*
for all exists within you
all around you comes
from your own breath

taste the mint leaf
you were the one who gave it sweetness
the smell of jasmine is your own scent

stop wasting your whole life seeking others
racing behind the parade like a panicked child
afraid no one will notice you

you are the parade
it is your panic that goes unnoticed
for the parade stops for no one's forlorn

you are not being left in the desert
you are the desert's leavings
golden sunset sacred silence horn

sip My hidden water and rise up
from this taunting earth

you are Glory's imagination
now imagine Glory
imagining you
gloriously.

Oranges in a wooden bowl
are to our eyes a nice arrangement
of separate things

look deeper
wooden bowl was once an orange tree

now mother holds her children.

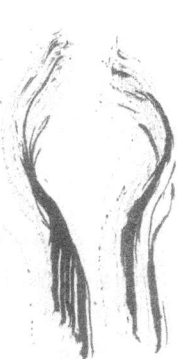

A dentist looks at you and sees
the gaps between your teeth

a doctor notices your pallor
a dermatologist your blemishes

all these practitioners see what
they are trained to see
and can correct those things

but none of them
can see the truth of you

only a soul guide can look at you
and see the gaping hole in the place
no one else can see

when the pangs of your void
strike you mercilessly
do not go chasing cures
from those equipped to attend
a different breed of pathology

instead be still and go silent
the true healers will come to you
like water from the mist

better yet they will come
at no charge and with no
appointment necessary

as long as you bow down naked
and empty in the river
they will be there
in the deepest water
pouring palms full over you

bow deep enough
and you may recognize
that the truest healer in the water
is your selfless self come
formless and faithful to take care of you.

Should you choose to be moon
your heavenly glow of face
will draw a world of attention

some will fall in Love with you
some will howl their great displeasure

for we live in a world of lesser lights
where eyes have grown comfortable
with the mediocrity of dimness

should you choose to be moon
the brightness of your face will startle
those who stumble in the dark

your light will take getting used to

even as you offer a clearer vision
many will want to remain in caves
content to gnaw on bones left over
from the cannibalizing of souls

they will snarl at your conspicuous aura
and each will pick up stones to cast at you

they will find their own reasons to slay you
achieving expertise at finding cause
devoting all their energy to knocking your
promissory lantern from the sky

their limbs will grow fatigued
then bloodied
then fall off

this will not stop them
they will pick up stones with their
jagged teeth and spit them at you
they will kick their legs off trying to
catapult rocks up against your lamp
of illuminated witness

when they exhaust themselves
they will curse you who brings the light
even as they cough into fits of breathlessness

astonishingly many of these howling souls
may be your own family and friends

though they Love you
they are bewildered by your light

you may feel betrayed and stung
but do not fret this hard stone
in your burlap bag of destiny

they have their own moon to reach
and be

for you that chance is now

be the moon
that dissuaded gem of light . . .

should you choose to be moon
know that you will inspire a world's vast
and conflicted response

the moment will be an aperture for revelation
look through that foreboding cleavage
into the radiance and see what is true:

as moon
those who cast against you
can never reach you
the distance is too far

only those who fall in Love
into your light
can reach you

and this is why moon shines steady
and unaffected through the night.

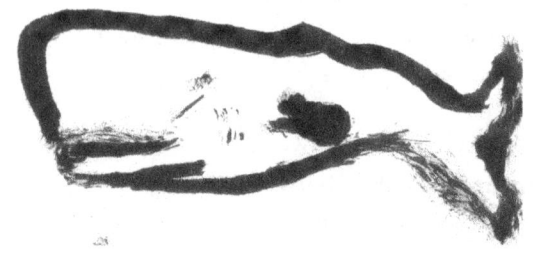

I have gathered a mountain
and filled it with Love
for you my friend

I have spilled that mountain
into the steeping sea
then poured that sea
into a gracious sky

with each pouring
Love's expansiveness
performed its nature
filling these willing jugs
each larger than the one before

this was not enough

with my deepest breath
I blew a warm and kindly gust
dispersing this sky of Love
into the unending universe

these are the errands
I have had to run
to find what could contain
the Abundance marinating
in my affection-gourd

minnows once swam
in my heart reservoir
then came you my friend
minnows changed to whales
and burst my insufficient aquarium

this explosive growth
forced my Love-tank to increase its size

now I go about Creation
seeking larger vessels
bigger barrels to stow this wine

such vintage resists stowing
longs only to be swallowed for thirst
quests for a new vineyard inside hearts

so gladly I break the glass
and spill my holding tank

all so that everywhere that *is*
this Heart-fire is too

for you my friend
for you.

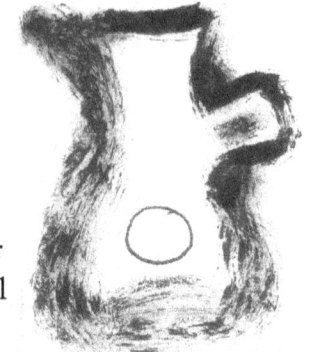

Shatter the glass pitcher
hoarding your sweet soul

cry out—wail—moan
bawl forth all your lake water
and smash the binding glass

only at this vulnerability
do your eagles wake
and hearing your surrender
take flight

coming with talons
to shred your tense identity
and take you the rest of the way
to drowning

your eagle-soul drops you perfectly
over waters made uniquely
for your soul cleansing

you plunge in
losing all aroma of the stockade and trough
to which you have been wed

bled of pungency
you open to a new fragrance
called *flowing*

before you is your own majesty
seated on the cracked stump of humility
resonating praise songs
inside an awesome curtain of light

you become the light raining
on your own song

you are the world looking on
at your own self in submission

Grace pours itself through you
in milk and honey

you are a fountain
and the bright air
the fountain water touches

you are the touching
and the birth from the touching

black birds dive from air rafters into you
dousing their fatigue in your watery plumage

resurrected they fly off to tell your story
in bold drafts of cawing

these blissful black birds are you
you have released them

you have released your heart and soul
from the carnage of intentional containment

now you are flight and voice
and endless volume
your glass shattered on the foamy
shoreline jaggedness of desolation

and you are your own angel
who chose to moan
and wail an invitation
to Grace
that it birth itself in you.

A million golden blades
make plush the meadow
within your heart

you already possess this peaceful garden
for which you have so long yearned

you need only lie down on this dreamy bed
of sun and softness to discover that you
have always been lighter
than the downy feather
freer than Forever
brighter than Creation's dawn

what you ache for
aches too for you

the world's great art holds its breath
until you cast your eyes its way

clay pots shaped
a thousand years before this day
were born for your particular admiration

their cracked bellies
pine for your Loving touch

your greatest dreams
are portraits you have stacked
for so long in deep dusty closets
now they bang on your inner doors

a certain ocean swoons for you
its coral blushing

cooing night sky
is filled with glowing lanterns
their paper skin
pulsing over candles' light

the finest wine flows
a river serpentine
through fields of flowers

the most magnificent expel their scent
clamor to be plucked by you

this is your life sweetening

pristine clouds give up their crystal water
for your growing thirst

as night alights on morning
vineyard valleys thick
of red and speckled berries
wake to thought of you
becoming fine and ready wine

ancient scrolls of sacred story
parchment duly lit
their obsidian ashes
lift high past mountain's reach
become music notes
blown from panoramic flute

become spices for your delicacy
lavender for your hot and lovely bath
ecstasy in the aftermath

you
heaving flute
billowing cascade of sighs

you
pulsing morning glory
wet calla lily petal
calcified burst of mineral
bequeathing your endurance
to the deep soak of Love

you
sultry streak of appetite
across gloaming sky

you
chariot arrived
quest incomplete
tidy offering to untidy wind
deep cave of laughter
awesome arc reclined
on brilliant pasture

chiseled notion
of high African plains
soapstone cheekbone
beneath red stone eye

dark maple river running
over a useful heart
playful spring sprung
from meander puddle

rain stick rattling
clouds agreeing

flower seed dancing
awestruck in ample air
fertile lips blowing
whisper so enticing
so undoing of these many bindings

you
who stops and kneels
to behold profound enormities
in the smallest play of soil and seed

you many nights
you warm willows that kindly bleed

you breath of orchid
you sculptured glory
you gown of moon

original blossom walking
nubile heart of rose exposed
unrepentant smile
packager of joy
planner of piñata bursting

you lapping tide
unchecked heart

you sufficient salt
you dampened river reed
you diffusing royal color
spilled to blush unliving stream

you endless rustle
of papyrus poetic pages

you swallower
of Beauty's conspired music

you belly full of stories told in food

you sacrament trees pour out in dew

you beaches burning
island beaming
jade parading creamy emerald
before sheets of swirling ivory

you walking ancestry
unfolded centuries
heavenly seasoned pot
of sumptuous stew

you scent of seven floral kisses
delightful sunning bouquet
tapestry woven by olive oiled hands

lair of passion pools
cave candlelit
shards of swift flicker
massaging rough cavern walls
into polished stone

you moaning discovery
you unbelievable moment
beneath the cypress trees

this poem can never end
it is carved from a tree whose
boundless girth
and rings of growth
are a carnival of infinity

you
the vintage in the air
that keeps the carnival
rejoicing.

INDEX OF FIRST LINES
(WITH NOTES)

Blinding white snow serves you sunlight   11
October 17, 2010

One wanderer asks another: 22
March 10, 2010. Meditating on sky.

In a simple moment   23
August 20, 2009. In bed, late on a cicada-songed summer night.

In this new light   26
January 3, 2010

A young monk goes walking   28
January 14, 2007

The young monk   30
January 11, 2007

Can your soul come out and play?   31
January 10, 2007

A bright sparrow brings you seeds of joy   35
February 10, 2007

You are walking in a cauldron of desert   37
August 23, 2010

With each breath   38
February 5, 2009

Catching butterflies is not like   39
January 1, 2009

Remember when we were walking   42
January 4, 2006

Peace is not a desire   44
January 5, 2007

You are blessed   45
January 5, 2007

Today Voci and I   46
January 6, 2007. While breathing deeply on a park bench in the sun. Seventy-plus degrees in a Maryland January! A celebration of Divine ancestral Friend, Voci, *The Voice*.

Two go walking   48
February 9, 2007

We stand in a river   50
February 9, 2009

A farmer wants the market vendor   50
December 22, 2005

Has the camel no right to purr   51
December 13, 2009

Sunlight opens the flower   52
November 24, 2008

A compassionate one tosses fitfully in bed   53
January 7, 2007

Excuse me 55
January 8, 2009

Sometimes our fears 55
January 10, 2000

A tree grows for 40 years 56
August 21, 2010

Decibels wave in desert silence 56
May 12, 2010. Celebration of the natural beauty of Joshua Tree National Park, and the stories it tells.

Here is what it means to be alive: 60
April 18, 2010

Self: 62
January 13, 2007

A willowy silent servant 63
January 16, 2010

A particular conversation occurs 66
September 16, 2010

In the soft nook of an old tree 67
January 19, 2010. Inspired by poetry from a friend.

A bright lotus grows brighter 70
November 24, 2008

Wishing for a blank white page of soul 71
December 16, 2009

If there is sun 73
January 23, 2004

A bow to Basho . . . 74
January 24, 2009 and July 9, 2009. At Pine Lake.
Matsuo Basho was a seventeenth century poet, known today as a *haisei*, the saint of haiku, and one of Japan's most renowned and revered writers. He was also a passionately itinerant traveler!

How many days in the whispering cave   77
January 24, 2009

A storyteller of caramel skin   79
January 28, 2005

If I have said this poem before   83
January 31, 2010

In the silence that dawns   86
January 31, 2010

We are a drunken spider   88
April 18, 2010

Endless pilgrimages to sit at the foot   91
March 31, 2009

Sometimes she finds a moment   93
February 8, 2009

To see our Truth   95
February 8, 2010

When we are truly flooded with Love   96
February 12, 2008

Great Spirit is blowing   98
February 18, 2007

A flower buds then blooms   99
February 27, 2010

Opportunity lies unseen in the dark   99
February 28, 2008

Life Loves us   103
March 13, 2003

Many moons have passed   104
March 15, 2009

Knowing that friend is dying to live   106
March 17, 2009

Fresh water perforates my banality   108
March 18, 2007

Under the baobab tree   109
March 18, 2008

Let's say you are suffering   112
March 20, 2009

Life greets us daily with a sublime   113
March 23, 2009

May the ground you walk   114
March 31, 2004

The Divine inscribes Itself   115
March 31, 2004

Do you remember the one   115
April 1, 2006

Some pray kneeling with palms   122
April 1, 2006

Have you read the Braille   123
April 1, 2009

How sweet the taste of sunrise   124
April 3, 2006

Sometimes   125
April 8, 2009. At Pine Lake.

Sky falls as water   125
April 11, 2010

Today I am Loving you   127
April 12, 2010

There is that which opens the heart   128
April 16, 2006. Easter.

Here is a meditation for you: 128
April 21, 2009

Decipher this: 129
April 22, 2010

Follow my voice old friend   130
April 28, 2009. On a chair of stones, by the sea (Mission Bay), moved by an all-night sharing with a Divine friend.

They greet in the courtyard   132
April 28, 2009. Inspired by a Divine friend.

A wandering monk encounters a soul   133
April 28, 2010

Another leaf drops gently onto lake   134
May 1, 2006

When no one is looking   135
May 2, 2009

When we encounter one who is suffering   136
May 28, 2010

That solemn heart pose   136
January 3, 2010

A note on true friendship: 137
May 23, 2010

Disrobe your Love   138
May 24, 2009

Willowy I say your name   140
May 24, 2009

You friend are a finder of things   141
May 24, 2009

You   142
August 10, 2010

Sky is another form of ocean   143
May 25, 2009

Remember when we were walking   145
May 31, 2010

Are you ready for the ocean of oceans?   146
June 5, 2010

Forest is a cane flute God's lips play   147
June 10, 2009

Why take a matter of your soul   148
September 16, 2010

Open your eyes friend   153
June 17, 2010

Those who assail us bless us   154
September 19, 2010

Dissolve into light and Love   155
November 24, 2008

When a thing catches fire   156
October 3, 2010

A lifelong musician shatters her instrument   159
June 21, 2006

Transient trawls a lantern across   161
June 25, 2010

Fear   163
June 26, 2003

A morning mantra for remembering: 164
July 6, 2008

If you find yourself frustrated   166
July 6, 2008

Sky speaks: 167
July 13, 2009

So many open windows . . .   169
July 24, 2009. For a Divine friend.

There are some things inside us   169
August 18, 2006

The conversation should always start with   170
September 2, 2008

We are so desperate to believe   170
October 2, 1989

Do not endeavor only to be a national treasure   171
December 13, 2009

Every   175
October 16, 2001

From the shelves of desert thrones   175
October 5, 1996

Wading into waters unknown   179
October 10, 2003. A version of this was previously published in Jaiya John's book *Beautiful*.

One seeker to another: 180
October 12, 2008

Love *is* life   182
October 20, 1997

You are a camel   183
October 29, 2007

Symbiosis: 184
November 1, 2008. At Brookside Gardens.

A new moment is born   184
November 8, 2009. At Pine Lake.

A poet composed his masterpiece   185
November 14, 2007

Become as the honeybee   187
November 18, 2008

Come   188
November 19, 2008

Sometimes it is enough simply to gaze   190
November 24, 2008

Peddler meets sojourner   191
November 27, 2007

Wisdom without compassion   194
November 18, 2004

Human Being   195
November 29, 1998

Fill your mind with flowers   198
December 7, 2006. In bed on a blue sky morning.

May you find those precious flowers   200
December 23, 2008

Shepherd reasons with a poor listener   201
September 25, 2010

In this country we need to practice smiling   203
December 10, 2006

Even a blade of grass   205
November 13, 2009. On the date of brother Greg's birthday.

Something without boundary   206
December 10, 2006

Oranges in a wooden bowl   209
December 13, 2006

A dentist looks at you and sees   209
December 13, 2009

Should you choose to be moon   211
December 13, 2009

I have gathered a mountain   214
November 9, 2010
In celebration of the birthday of a beloved friend.

Shatter the glass pitcher   216
December 28, 2009

A million golden blades   218
June 25, 2007

Jaiya John was born and raised in New Mexico, and has lived in various locations, including Nepal. He fills his life with relationship, writing, speaking, and supporting young lives. He is the founder of Soul Water Rising, a global human mission.

Jacqueline V. Richmond and Kent W. Mortensen graciously and skillfully served as editors for *Lyric of Silence*.

Jaiya John titles are available where books are sold. Book revenue supports our *Young Life Drumbeat* youth development programming, including our scholarship and book donation programs for displaced and vulnerable youth.

Other Books by Jaiya John

To learn more about this and other books by Jaiya John, to order discounted bulk quantities, or to learn about Soul Water Rising's global work, please visit us at:

soulwater.org

jaiyajohn.com

facebook.com/jaiyajohn

itunes (search: jaiya john)

youtube.com/soulwaterrising

@jaiyajohn (Instagram & twitter)

To subscribe to our literary journal, *SOUL BLOSSOM*, please visit soulwater.org.

Soul Blossom is a literary journal, offering ongoing news of our global human mission, new book release notices, speaking engagement insights, and invited literary contributions.

Soul Blossom is also a gathering space for the writing and artwork of young people from around the world.

www.ingramcontent.com/pod-product-compliance
Lightning Source LLC
Chambersburg PA
CBHW020836160426
43192CB00007B/673